COPYRIGHT

FRUGAL SPENDING: HOW TO LIVE FRUGALLY ON A TIGHT BUDGET

No part of this book or eBook should be reproduced, transmitted, downloaded, decompiled, reverse engineered, or restored in or introduced into any information storage and retrieval system, in any form, or by any means. Whether it is electronic or mechanical, now know or hereinafter invented without the expressed written of the copyright owner.

This is a work of real life places and incidents, which are used to inspire, encourage, and help others through different areas of transitioning financially. These are experiences through the authors' real life.

The reverse engineering and uploading of Books or eBooks via internet or any other means without permission of the copyright owner is illegal and punishable by law.

Please purchase Paperback or eBook only authorized.

Your support of the author's rights are appreciated.

Book

FRUGAL SPENDING:HOW TO LIVE FRUGALLY ON A TIGHT BUDGET –   VOLUME 2

ISBN-10: 1533433208

ISBN-13: 978-1533433206

Author: Bridget C. Williams

Publisher: CreateSpace Independent Publishing Platform ((May 23, 2016)

Copyright©2016 Bridget C. Williams

All rights reserved.

Bridget Williams

Table of Content Page

GETTING BACK TO BASICS	2
FRUGAL MEANS	4
DATING TIPS	7
ENTERTAIN YOURSELF	11
GOALS	14
ORGANIZING YOUR LIFE	20
CHALLENGES TO SAVE MONEY	26
HOBBIES	33
FOOD STRETCHING	47
INEXPENSIVE FOOD	52
SALADS & SALAD DRESSINGS	54
FREE THINGS OR RECYCLED ITEMS	70
REBATES	81
ORGANIZING	89
IMPULSE SHOPPING/RETAIL THERAPHY	100
CONSIGNMENT VS. PAWNSHOP	105
BECOMING A MINAMALIST	109
THE CONFESSION OF A SHOPAHOLIC	115
FROM SHOPAHOLIC TO HOARDER	120

Adjusting and transitioning is difficult but taking baby steps does work.

When you are on a fixed income trying to raise a family, student, senior, or just a family with a low-high income, or just want to get back on track financially... FRUGAL is the way to go.   However, you don't have to have a low income to take advantage of savings and have smart Money Management. Money Management is tough for all levels of finances. Try to save as much as you can for those emergencies that come up. The first thing is recognizing how much money you spend by creating a budget and taking a debt free program.   On my journey of getting out of debt it is truly a struggle still but baby steps are better than know steps.   I also had to do this with little money and casual work. I had realized that I had a problem and starting to do research on ways to save money, by watching shows, videos, taking a class, and trying to adapt these tips into my life.   I always wondered why they didn't teach this in school because so many of us would be in a better predicament today.

GETTING BACK TO BASICS

Traditionally, I remember my grandparents living off the land, passing 2nd hand clothes to the siblings, making gifts instead of buying gifts, cooking instead of buying all process foods, handmade decorations for the Christmas tree, and helping others in the community, and so much more.   Those were the days when people live more frugal and didn't allow consumerism to consume them. They only purchased what was necessary and didn't waste money.

The toughest thing about getting out of debt is trying to change behaviours and attitude and acknowledge that there is a serious problem.

When I became consumer struck... it was my teenage years when I had my 1st job and new that I could buy what I wanted and spent a ridiculous amount of money on things for years.   *Spending money was retail therapy for me instead of dealing with problems– I shopped as my outlet.   It's pretty bad when you walk in stores and they know you by name and classify you as a VIP customer.*   I am certain that there are so many of you in the same situation.   Living outside your means from pay check to pay check is a crazy way to live.   The money that was wasted on things could have been put to retirement, education, emergency fund, and so much more.   I should have, could have, but didn't because I didn't know better.

FRUGAL AND TRANSITIONING

Thanking god for seeing brighter days and for making it possible, to transition into a life of frugal spending is a journey within itself. Starting over and New Beginnings is a life changing transformation no matter where you are in life.
I look at my needs vs. my wants and can truly say that my mind will start saying is that a need or want. I end up putting things back which is huge for me. Maintaining frugal changes can be complex but takes practice.
I created a monthly budget which helps me with my spending. I can now see where the money is going and can make the necessary adjustments. I have to keep challenging myself in order for this to work. I continue to look for free or very inexpensive ways to do things for making necessary purchases. ***When you hear people say I am not out of debt yet***….Well what are you doing about it? If you sitting around not making the modifications/changes or incorporating what you learned it's not going to work. Life style changes and choices must be made, this is not a race. It takes time and due diligence in order for this to work. You may have to repeat the practice over and over again until you get it right.

My goal is to be a financial steward and be happy. You don't have to spend money for everything. There are so many free things that people are not aware of. I will dialogue about those things throughout this webpage.
This is very important. Sometimes you have to be selfish and do things for yourself. Whatever it is that makes you happy, do more of it as long as it's free, frugal, or planned for. Get your finances in order so you can fully benefit from this blessing.

There is a section called Inventory of your life and positive impact to help you reflect on yourself and others (**Adjusting Your Life Style and New Beginnings Book 1**). There are many ways of handling situations and circumstances. This is food for the soul.

Bridget Williams

Frugal Spending

Bridget Williams

FRUGAL LIVING MEANS

IT TIME TO MAKE NECESSARY CHANGES!

So . . . you've decided to give the frugal life a shot, and now you're wondering what you've committed to. Does frugal living mean dooming yourself to a life of deprivation, just so you can save a few cents here and there?

Frugal living isn't about sacrifice and deprivation; it's about living smarter, so that you can afford to live the life that *you* want to live – the life that *you* dream of living.

Frugal living means Smart Money Management.

When you know how much money you have in the bank and how much money you need to cover your monthly bills, you can begin to make better decisions about how your money is spent. Avoid splurging the money can be used for an emergency or when you actually need to use it for necessities.

Is this the right time to buy a new car? Put a frugal budget in place, and you'll know just what you can afford, and more importantly, what you can't afford.

Investments—a key step to taking charge of your money and making it work for you – take the ***Debt free program with Jason Vaillancourt*** and acquire the necessary skills and tips on investments and money management.

Frugal living means smarter spending.

It's taking the money that you have and *stretching* it as far as it will go.

It's learning how to get the best deal on everything that you buy— shopping thrift stores, yard sales, clearance racks and barter boards until you find what you want at a price that you can afford; using coupons and rebates in combination with sales to get the very best price on your groceries; and perhaps even stockpiling items when you find them at an unbeatable price. **It's also knowing when *not* to shop** – holding off on a purchase that doesn't fit into your budget, and patiently waiting for a sale to bring an item down to your price. When you adopt the habits of a frugal shopper, you are in full control of your spending.

Frugal living means harnessing your creativity.

It's about finding ways to make do with what you have, and learning how to do more for yourself.

Do you pay someone to change your oil, or do it yourself? Sew a patch on a pair of holey jeans, or buy a new pair? Purchase trash bags, or reuse your plastic grocery bags?

Every day presents new opportunities to reuse, re-purpose and create, and it's the frugal person who recognizes those opportunities, seizes them and turns them into savings

Why Live Frugally?

Okay, so frugal living is about better money management, bargain shopping and creativity, but what does all of that add up to? Can these three things really result in a better life?

Absolutely.

Frugal living unlocks a world of possibilities. Want to pay off all of your debts? Fund your child's education? Enjoy the security of a fat bank account? Travel the world?

You can make it happen.

Frugal living is about determining what you want out of your life, and finding a way to make it happen. A couple dollars saved here, and a few dollars invested there doesn't translate into a life of deprivation; it translates into possibilities. Decide what you want to get out of life, and then use frugality to make it happen.

FUN FRUGAL DATING

The point of going on frugal dates isn't just to "go out and do stuff," but to make sure you keep the activities not only frugal, but fun and special.

Honestly, it doesn't matter what you spend as long as you make it a focus on connection and making the ordinary moments into memorable ones.

- *Go to a drive in movie – you can take your own food.*
- *Visit your local botanical gardens or park to see the spring bulbs, bring a camera*
- *Attend a local spring festival or local farmer's market (Google it for a variety of options!)*
- *Plan a spring brunch with other couples, or just one on one*
- *Take in free community activities*
- *Go on an Easter egg hunt (feel free to do an adult version!)*
- *Rent some wheels and go on a tour via bicycle*
- *Go hiking or for a long city walk to see new points of interest*
- *Take a drive to another city to explore the local scene in spring*
- *Visit a local winery or grab a deal for day long winery excursions*
- *Grab a Groupon and enjoy eating outdoors to try a new local restaurant*
- *Set up a day to take pictures together while the flowers are blooming*
- *Go to a baseball game together (when tickets are cheaper!)*
- *Get into running and train for a 5k together*
- *Eat around the world (try new restaurants or cook at home) for a day*

- *Scope out free/cheap weekend classes at the library or community college for nifty adventures in arts & crafts, gardening, local culture and home improvement*
- *Explore a new neighbourhood or neighbouring town*
- *Visit your local farmer's markets*
- *Make mix CDs or playlists for one another*
- *Go for a picnic*
- *Grab a blanket and watch a meteor shower*
- *Check out local movies or concerts in the park*
- *Go hiking in a new place, bring a camera*
- *Bring a camera and spend all day taking pictures somewhere new*
- *Learn to cook something new for summer on the grill or campfire*
- *Rent or borrow a bike and go for a long ride*
- *Find a fire pit at your local park or beach and make smores for a night picnic*

- *Cook your family recipes for one another & share the stories behind them*
- *Head to the beach or lake and enjoy the weather*
- *Visit a summer faire or festival that offers free admission*
- *Grab discount passes for your local aquarium or zoo*
- *Attend free tastings by your favorite breweries or distilleries*
- *Join a local amateur sports team together*
- *Help one another fix up your digs, home improvement pizza*
- *Take a lunch date at work (even if it means going out of your way)*
- *Drive to find the best spot to watch the sunset together*
- *Go for a walk to try all the best ice cream spots within walking distance*
- *Go bowling on a weeknight*
- *Take dance lessons together (after finding a good deal!)*
- *Take a fall road trip just to see the fall colors*
- *Go apple picking*

- *Locate an arcade, stock up on quarters and have as much fun as humanly possible*
- *Find a pumpkin patch & enjoy the festivities*
- *Go watch a local football game*
- *Carve pumpkins & decorate for fall*
- *Have cheesy Halloween movie marathon complete with themed snacks*
- *Try to create your signature cocktail, then after a few, come up with a name*
- *Paint your own ceramics (even better if it's BYOB too!)*
- *Clean out your closets with your own at-home fashion show (champagne encouraged)*
- *Go back to the place you had your first date, even it's not your anniversary*
- *Play like kids at your local park, crunch around in the fall leaves*
- *Have another couple over for a game night*
- *Have a wine tasting night at home (try different whites or reds to learn your favourites)*
- *Have a beer tasting night at home (taste around the world, learn different styles)*
- *Walk around & take pictures together or of one another*
- *Do a trial run of Thanksgiving for just the two of you- no fussy relatives invited*
- *Go to the Dollar Store & go on a gift scavenger hunt for $5 each*
- *Enjoy a day of mini golfing & a round of go-karts*
- *Check out books at the local library to discover & cultivate new interests*
- *Rent bad movies and get snarky Mystery Science Theater 3000 style, best snark wins a prize*

- *Make a scrapbook of your favourite memories together*
- *Learn how to make bread (it's a great excuse to eat wine & cheese too!)*

- *Plan your holiday gifts for family and friends & create them together*
- *Go on a cheesy movie marathon (70's, 80's 90's are great decades!)*
- *Find local holiday markets and go browse*
- *Play your favourite board games or video games from childhood (pair with your favourite foods)*
- *Write out your bucket list and share ideas*
- *YouTube a new skill & learn together (cooking, home improvement, massage?)*
- *Pop open some champagne and plan your New Year's goals together*
- *Dress up for a night in- even if you're eating in, make it special*
- *Plan a romantic meal where both people cook and you indulge in finery from home*
- *Go play in the snow like kids. Make snowmen, snow angels and maybe a snowball fight?*
- *Make ornaments or decorations to commemorate your year together*
- *Volunteer together for a cause you care about*
- *Make traditional holiday recipes that you've never attempted before to establish new traditions*
- *Revel in the toy aisle to act like a kid again, then buy something for Toys For Tots*
- *Find an ice skating rink & finish up with hot cocoa*
- *Make a time capsule to open together next year*
- *Sit down and take time to tell each other your family stories and the history of your family tree*
- *Snuggle up to all the holiday movies you can find and make adult hot cocoa*
- *Start your own two person book club...with wine (obviously)*
- *Explore new music together set a theme and listen*
- *Play a video games together that are geared to storytelling or team play*
- *Roaring fireplace, find one. The rest will solve itself*
- *Create envelopes for each month of the year and write love notes to each other to be opened each month in the new year.*

REMEMBER IT'S NOT ABOUT THE MONEY. IT'S ABOUT THE TIME AND MEMORIES CREATED.

ENTERTAINING YOURSELF WITH OUT SPENDING MONEY

Invite friends over. The best way to spend time and not money: Invite friends over just to hang out and talk!

Attend a free event. If you live in a major city or near a college there are probably free events happening all the time. Look online for community calendars and check at the local library for listings of free events.

Write a letter to a friend. Getting real mail is rare these days so it has become extra special. Make someone's day by writing and mailing a letter.

Call your mom. No matter how old you are your mom (or other special person) will always love to hear from you. Give her a call and tell her about your life and remember to say I love you.

Write a letter to your representative. We all have causes we care about. Take the time to write a letter to your representative to voice your opinion on an issue. Plus it's election time so this stuff matters!

Read a blog. Browse new posts and dig through the archives of a good blog for a few hours. Here's a list of personal finance blogs I like.

Write a blog post. Write something for your own blog or another blog about a topic you are passionate about. Don't have a blog yet? Start a blog NOW.

Organize your things. Go through a room and organize the items in it. Throw away old things; straighten up, make things look nice.

Organize your photos. Go through your photo library and organize everything and order prints. Put printed photos in albums and frames.

De-clutter your house. Work room through to get rid of extra clutter and errant items.

Sell your stuff on Craigslist. All that stuff you found during organizing and de-cluttering? Put it up on Craigslist for sale! This is a great free activity because it will actually earn you money!

Yard Sale. Anything that doesn't sell on Craigslist or is too small to be sold there can be offered up in a yard sale. You can advertise for free and potentially make a few hundred dollars on the venture.

GOALS

WHY DO YOU WANT TO BECOME FRUGAL

To get started, let's think about YOUR reason to make a frugal fresh start. It's probably not just for the fun of it, or to get attention from your friends. Maybe you want to pay off those credit cards once and for all. Maybe you want to save for a house. Maybe your retirement accounts are slimmer than you'd like. Maybe you just have a spending problem. Who couldn't use a little more cash in their pockets?

Let's turn your reason for wanting to spend less, into a goal.

SETTING GOALS

This can change things enormously and by staying on track. If you are not one of those people who have set up Financial Goals for yourself, you might be someone who is wondering aimlessly because you have nothing to strive for. Setting goals gives you something to work toward and this can be a very rewarding aspect of your life. Setting financial goals for you is no different than setting a personal goal.

Maybe you have a goal weight you are working toward or you maybe you want to be an artist so you are taking classes to reach that goal. This is the same thing for your finances, you can begin by putting a list together, your goals, and then be as specific as possible. You also want to be prepared for life's emergencies so you purchase insurance. If you were to be part of an accident that was not your fault, you could file an accident claim so you could collect compensation.

A plan of action is what is needed to be able to stay in **CONTROL YOUR FINANCES**. Your list of goals must be both realistic and specific and then you will need to prioritize your list if it is a long one. Some goals are more important than others. You might decide that one can wait but another needs to be started on now.

Adjustments can be made where needed so you end up with a list that is doable. You will also want to review your progress to see if you are indeed meeting your goals. You might set yourself a GOALS **TO SAVE** for a down payment on a home or to pay cash for a new car, just make sure your saving account is an interest earning account. It is the compound interest that will help you to reach those goals faster and that is what we all want, fast results to the work we do. Good luck with your goals, and never give up.

BE REALISTIC– It's important to have small, incremental goals to build your way to the ultimate one.

KNOW YOURSELF-It's very, very hard to change who you are. You can make little tweaks here and there.

CHECK IN REGULARLY -Financial goals are only possible if you regularly monitor them.

WHY PEOPLE DON`T REACH GOALS

Goals are an integral part of how most successful people reach the heights they do. It is *very* rare that someone will say, "I became incredibly successful and I wasn't even trying to accomplish anything." In fact, I would argue that there is no pure triumph without goals, effort, and dedication.
It can feel like your dreams have gone up in smoke if you never make any progress. But I always believe there's a way to overcome failure.

▪ LACK OF FOCUS

This is the number one problem for people who never seen to be able to accomplish their goals. If you don't adjust your attitude and change your ways you will be stuck in a rut.
Think of how detailed your number one hope or dream is. Answer yourself honestly about whether it is realistic or even well defined. Here is an example of lack of focus by not adjusting the attitude/focus.
Lack of Focus: **I want to stop shopping**…. You really need to look at is the purchasing a need or a want. If it`s not necessary don`t buy it.
You want to lose weight but continue to eat junk and unhealthy foods.

The first example isn't really considered a true goal at all. It's a wish, a hope, an idea. A realistic goal is a clear, well-defined target that anyone can reach, even if it initially seems unattainable. But they must start with believing in themselves and focus!

▪ NO ACCOUNTABILITY

For the sake of this post, let's pretend you want to reach the goal listed above and lose 30 pounds by a certain date by exercising and eating healthier. So you start jogging every day and buying overpriced from specialty stores or elaborate Grocery stores.   By foods frugally and watch your intake of sugar and salt. But then life gets a little hectic and you buy one snack size bag of candy for an extra boost in energy. No big deal, right? I mean, it was just a bag of candy and who would find out anyway? *That's the problem!*

You're more likely to stick to your goals if you have a partner doing it with you can monitor each other. You need someone to turn to and confide in if you start to lose your confidence.

▪ NO TIME-FRAME

Expectations often become realities through hard work and deadlines. Set a realistic target date and work towards it. To ensure your development/transition is staying on track check your numbers frequently this will help during your progress.

As part of human nature we will sometimes respond very well to expectations. You'll be more inclined to work hard and stay focused if you have a deadline.

▪ DISTRACTIONS

There is usually something more entertaining to do than the undertaking of complicated goals. But if you spend all that time wishing and not working towards your goal, you may never get there.

Stay focused by writing out a step by step plan. Then be sure to complete these tasks *in order*! Don't jump around at random and get distracted. You've got this. Just stay focused.

▪ YOU'RE LISTENING TO NEGATIVE INFLUENCES

One of the best ways to cheat on your diet is to hang out with someone who doesn't believe you have the willpower to lose weight and baked you a cake to prove it.

Negative comments like "I don't know if you can do this," or "It's okay if you just give up," are things that you don't need to hear.

No, it's not the end of the world if you never reach your goals. But don't be convinced that you'll never cross the finish line before you even start the race.

▪ THERE'S A LACK OF MEASURABILITY

We all need a little encouragement when the going gets rough. Taking note of the progress you've made is the perfect incentive to keep up the good work. Remember when you listed all of your goals with a deadline in number 3? Start keeping track of how close you are to completing each step. Continuously ask yourself, "Where am I compared to yesterday? Am I making progress or falling behind?"

▪ YOU'RE TOO HARD ON YOURSELF

Negative influences can really make or break your self-esteem. Other people may say negative things to you but you should also consider whether *you* are being too hard on yourself.

Do you beat yourself up for failing to reach small targets? Or do you give yourself a pep talk to overcome the challenges you're facing? Be determined in your efforts but also be your own number one cheerleader.

▪ NOTHING IS WRITTEN DOWN

This weakness ties in with the first problem I listed. Where there's a lack of focus, there's usually no written structure.

Taking pen to paper (or computer ink to computer paper) will sometimes trick our brains into thinking our goals are more realistic. You can hang them up above your desk or on your refrigerator. They act as a constant reminder of who you want to be, where you're going, and how you're going to get there.

▪ YOU FOCUS ON EVERYTHING AND NOTHING AT ALL

Do you know the phrase "spreading yourself too thin?" Say that you've created a list of 10 things you should do to eat healthier, exercise, and eventually lose weight. Do you focus on one step at a time or do you try to finish all ten at once? As tempting as it is to dive right in and power through everything, you'll go much further by being patient and making progress one step at a time.

▪ YOUR GOALS ARE NOT YOUR OWN

Spend the next few minutes thinking about your top ten hopes and dreams. What do they look like? How do they change your life? Does the idea of seeing them come true make you smile?

How can you pour 100% of your being into a goal that is not even your own? Let's go back to the example we talked about before. Are you losing 30 pounds for yourself or for someone else?

▪ YOU'RE NOT BEING PATIENT

Be patient with your work and you'll often find things operating more efficiently. If you rush past all of your duties, you'll miss important details or steps that can hurt your progress later on.

I've taken on large projects thinking, "If I can just quickly work through this I know I'll see results in no time!" Nine times out of ten I either failed or didn't put in my best work because I was in a hurry.

Did any of these problems sound familiar to you? If the answer is yes, you are not alone! I wouldn't be able to write about them if I hadn't made the mistakes myself.

ORGANIZING OUR LIFE

Find free stuff. If you happen to need items rather than getting rid of them, sign up for curb alert groups and browse Craigslist and Freecycle for free items.

Rearrange your furniture. Change up your living room and try new furniture configurations. Try something new and see if you like it. I'm doing this one since I just got new furniture!

Clean your house. Scrub the bathroom, floors, windows, everything. Make the house the cleanest it's ever been, or at least in a while.

Clean your car. Clean out all the junk that accumulates in a car and give it a nice wash inside and out. Make it look like a million bucks.

Do some yard work. Cut your grass, trim the shrubs, rake the leaves. Manual labour is free and productive. You'll be able to enjoy the landscaping for many months or years after!

Make a to-do list. Make a list of all the things you need to do and have been putting off. They might cost money but making the list doesn't!
Tackle a nagging task. Tackle one of the pesky lingering tasks always on your to-do list and cross it off forever.

Go for a walk or run. Explore your neighbourhood or a new part of town by foot. See things from a new perspective and get exercise.

Go for a bike ride. Check out the trails or popular bike routes in your city.

Go for a hike. Explore the nature near you by hiking in the woods.

Try an at home exercise challenge. Do the 100 push-ups or 100 sit-ups challenge. It's free, fun, and challenging!

Test out a new gym for free. Almost every gym out there offers a free trials period. Test out a new gym and change up your work-out for the week.

Enjoy the sun. One of the nicest things to do on a sunny day is to spend time outside walking or stretch out. Be sure to use sunscreen while you gloriously bask in the sun for free.

Gaze at the stars. A free night time activity involves a blanket, no lights, and your eyes. Go find a secluded place and just rest and watch the big beautiful universe.

Take a nap. Relax for a bit and let your body rest. Naps as an adult can be glorious!

Take a bath. Sure water isn't really free, but you have to get clean anyway! Take a relaxing warm bath at home and enjoy the little luxuries.

Try a new hairstyle. Create a list of hairstyles you would like to try out and attempt one. It might take a few tries to get right so your time will be well spent creating a new look for yourself.

Try a new outfit. Chances are you only wear a percentage of your closet and even that is worn in the same way. Try out some new looks with the clothes you already have be trying new combinations and accessories. Shop your closet!

Mend your clothes. You most likely have a pile of clothes to mend or hem that you'll get to "sometime" in the future. Tackle the clothes that need a little TLC and restore your wardrobe to its glory days.

Host a clothing swap. Host a party where friends come over and bring items they want to give up to get other items. You all save money and get free new items to wear.

Read a book. Curl up with a good book and you'll have a free adventure that lasts for hour or days. Hit up your library or Amazon's free eBooks list. Here's the top 100 free eBooks on Amazon.

READ·A·BOOK

Write something. Use your imagination and create a story or draft a blog post or jot down old memories.

Write a list of reasons not to spend money. Write a list of reasons why you want to save rather and spend and put your future goals in writing. It will motivate you to do all the things on this list rather than spend money!

Babysit. Sure teens use babysitting as a way to make money , but it's also a nice gift you can give new parents. Offer to watch their kids for free as a sweet thing to do. It also can be fun!

Make a card. Get crafty and use the materials around your house to make a card for an upcoming holiday or just because. You can even stockpile these and use them throughout the year.

Make gifts. Christmas is coming and birthdays go year round. Check out easy DIY gift guides for ideas and use what you already have to make cute gifts for friends and family.

Make a pinterest pin. Most of us have a pinterest account with hundreds of pinned ideas. Take the time to make one of those pins with the supplies you already own.

Go on a photo scavenger hunt. Take your camera or just your phone and complete a photo scavenger hunt around your area. You can make up your own list of items to find or borrow one from an existing website.

Take a pantry recipe challenge. Challenge yourself to use what is in your pantry to create a new and exciting dinner for your family.

Create a meal plan. Write out your meals for the next week or month. Getting organized is free and will also save you money on groceries and eating out in the long run.

Potluck. Make that new pantry dish or another that you have ingredients for and have others come over to provide the rest of the meal. Potlucks are always a fun and inexpensive way to get together with people.

 Watch a new show. Check out the free shows on hulu or most network channel websites. Pick a show and watch a new episode or two.

Host a TV or movie marathon. Invite friends over and collectively pull together a marathon based on shows and movies you already own. Try to base it around a theme or genre for a more cohesive evening.

Check your finances. Take a few hours and do your annual review of your finances. Look at your spending levels, adjust your budget, review your investments. Use Personal Capital to get an overview of your finances and make adjustments as necessary.

Write out your future goals. Nothing is more motivating than dreaming. Take some time to dream about your life and write down the major things you want to achieve. Give yourself the free time to decide what you really want out of life. Figuring out your life goals might just inspire you to make a big change.

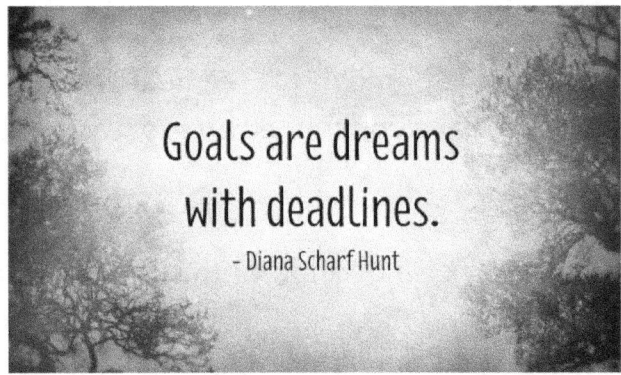

Write a gratitude list. One thing I love to do when I'm feeling restless and wanting to spend/buy/consume is to make a list of what I already have. Listing out what you have and what you are grateful for reminds you that life is wonderful and you already have a lot. It also gives you something to do without spending money!

Volunteer. Volunteering is free except for your time and it's extremely rewarding. You can find volunteer positions online.

Leave positivity where you go. It's free to offer a smile or leave a positive note in a library book. Look for ways during your day to impart kindness and happiness among those cross.

CHALLENGES TO SAVE MONEY

These are challenges to help you save money and get out of debt. Start with one at a time and see what works best for you.

1. SEAL THE POT CHALLENGE

Get a bottle and put $10 – $50 per week or $5(hardship). Do not use any of the money for one year. You be amazed how much money you can save.

2. MAKE EXTRA MONEY CHALLENGE

Finding a second job, online surveys, Mystery Shopping, set weekly challenges and keep track of all your money.

3. JUNKFOOD CHALLENGE

No purchasing junk food, bars, chips, juice, all types of snacks, including deserts. You will save so much money and may lose weight also from not inhaling these items.

4. **52 WEEK CHALLENGE**

This challenge you have to put $50, $100, $150, each week the amount increases for you to put into a jar and not spend.   Do it —you will surprise you, and make it a contest with family and friends. You have to be truly disciplined to do this.

5. **TAKE YOUR LUNCH TO WORK CHALLENGE**

Take food from home and refreshments. Do not purchase any fast food items or beverages?   The money you would normally spend put in a Jar.

6. **TRACKING ALL OF YOUR RECEIPTS CHALLENGE**

Keep track of all receipts and record your spending.   You will be amazed at how much spending on certain items you waste money on.   This will teach you how to cut back on your spending and look at the importance of needs vs. wants. Make a budget and record all expenses you will be surprised how things can add up. ***Learn from this and make the necessary adjustments.***

7. **NO PURCHASING GROCERIES CHALLENGE**

You must eat all the food in your cupboards, refrigerator, and freezer before you buy any food. Look at the money you save by not making unnecessary purchases. The money you save from not purchasing groceries can be used for the next grocery trip. ***Start the process again…. You save more money when you're not in the stores every day or week***.

8. **PAYMENT A DAY CHALLEGE**

The principle of the idea is that you pay any extra money you have against a debt to clear it a little bit quicker. Not everyone makes a daily payment, but instead they save money to make a lump sum at the end of the month. You can do it anyway you want to. It is a great way to pay off your debt.

9. **ELECTRICY/POWER CHALLENGE**

Turn off lights when not in use. During summer turn off breakers and heaters that are not being used. Unplug electronics when not being used. Get a power bar for computers and Televisions, games, which are being used.   Light bulbs change to power smart light bulbs. ***Start looking at more power smart ways to save money.***

Look into **Power Smart Savings** for water and electricity contact your power and water company for tips.

10. PAY CHECK CHALLENGE

Each month put one check aside for bills and save the other check for future savings. Watch your money grow... this will help you for emergencies. Only use it if you absolutely have to.

11. GAS CHALLENGE

Avoid driving all over the place make one trip to go to work, shopping, picking up kids, etc. The money you spend on gas will decrease which is a huge savings. Also buddy up with someone to save cost for you and the other person. You can also use transit periodically. Look at how much it cost to drive vs. taking transit. Biking is another method during the summer month.

12. BOTTER WATER CHALLENGE

Don't buy bottle water use water from your home. Boil water before refrigeration. If it tastes bad infuse it with fruits, or lemons, mint, etc.

13. FLYER CHALLENGE

Only use grocery flyer... put the rest in the garbage. Consumers want you to spend because of sales, and deals, and more, to entice you to spend.

14. CLOTHING CHALLENGE

This is to challenge you to shop at second hand stores like frenchees, and other **2nd hand stores**. Have a set amount prior to shopping. You can find unused clothing (**new**) for cheap. **Clothes swamping** with your female friends and family are great prospects. If you sew... make clothes with unused fabrics. If the stores has a sale on do not spend over $1-$10 per item. It's safe to budget before leaving home and only take cash. Sometimes the SECOND hand stores have $2 sales on. **THIS IS NOT A LICENSE TO GO SHOPPING.**

15. COUPON CHALLENGE

This is tough for some people. Start using coupons when shopping for groceries, cleaners, clothing, and save when available. Small saving will add up—every bit counts.

16. GROCERY LIST CHALLENGE

When you go groceries shopping a lot of people don't make up a grocery list prior to shopping. It's time to make up a grocery list for purchases. Whatever is not on the list don't pick up. Some people will do this in groups and do bulk shopping this will save a lot of money. You can start with family members include your kids (*this is training for them*)... and break up into groups of 2, and designate certain items for each group to pick up. You will have fun and also save money.

Don't forget your coupons!

17. NO CREDIT CARD USE CHALLENGE

If you have credit cards put them into a safe place that you can't get to right away. Using cash only is huge and very difficult. Taking baby steps will help you immensely.

It's about practicing, and if you don't have cash don't buy it. Save up for things that you want…. and plan ahead.

Have you planned your menu for the week?

18. MEAL PLANNING CHALLENGE

This can be done with family and friends. You buy your meats vegetables, pasta, and more. Creating meals for the week can help save you from going out to purchase. It's a great way to save. Try it with neighbours and family members.   Decide on the menu for the week. Once you decided follow the below information.

For example:

- Cut up meat, fish, or other (opt out with beans, or other protein if you are vegetarian)
- Cut up vegetables
- Pasta, rice, potatoes, bean, or other.
- Spices
- Sauce

Get into assembly line and bag your items, per meal, it fun and a great way to spend time with family.   You can prepare the meals for the week, or just have items ready to cook daily. Prepping your meal in advance is a great way to save time and money.

Try it you'll like it!

INEXPENSIVE HOBBIES

Hobbies

Think you have to spend money to have fun? **This is not true.**
Living on a really tight budget because you want to get out of debt or just save money or retire early doesn't have to mean sitting in a dark room eating noodles. It just means doing inexpensive hobbies. Even better, you might find a few that pay you to do them.

Spirituality

Simplifying your life is going without: Having said that, you will appreciate what you do have and will think differently, it can improve your will power significantly.

Minimalism: Get rid of your possessions that own you and get happy.

Yoga: relaxing

Investigate Religion: Whether it's so you know more about a religion you don't follow, or to   know more about the one you do.

Find a Church: Go to a church that you feel connected with. **New Beginnings Ministries -26 Cherry Brook Rd., Cherry Brook, Nova Scotia Canada or our new North Dartmouth location** is a great Church for starting over or just to have a spiritual experience, with lovely kindred individuals.

Church Programs: If you want to grow in your faith and spirituality take the classes that the church offers. It will be beneficial to you in your growth.

Philosophy: the study of the fundamental nature of knowledge, reality, and existence, especially when considered as an academic discipline.

Meditation: Not doing anything at all for long periods while deeply contemplating life or nothing at all is probably the ultimate frugal pastime!

Prayer Wall: Pray for intervention and for release over your circumstances.

Intellectual

 Reading: Reading can educate you about the world or grip you with an amazing tale. You probably have a library near you that is full of good books available for free.

Writing: You only need a computer or a pen and paper. Whether you like writing letters to the others or want to work on writing the novel you're not going to spend much money in the process. During your process of becoming frugal you should write down what you want to accomplish and what your current state is.   Just check off each item as you progress.

Self-Assessment is something I do yearly where I am, and what would I like to see change, spirituality, creation, plan of actions, and obtainable goal setting. Your mindset has to be in place of empowerment when you take this on because only you know your situation.

Drawing: Painting, sketching, doodling or being creative with a pencil. Drawing is one of the cheapest ways to pass the time.

Learn a language: There are a plethora of wonderful free resources available online to help you learn a language. You can listen to podcasts on the way to work or work through a structured course. Soon enough you'll be speaking French.

Podcasts: Learn a language, listen to your favourite comedian, listen to a great documentary or catch up on the latest news. **Podcasts are an awesome source of information and are (by and large) free!**

Educate yourself: Learn how to do things—make it a project. Do an open course for free. *Read Wikipedia*. Learning about the world is fun and will make you a better person.

Exercise

Running: Then running is the exercise equivalent. You can do it almost anywhere and you only need decent sneakers. There is always something to improve on, races to enter or just to stay in shape.

Swimming: Not necessarily cheap if you can only do it at a swimming centre with inexpensive membership. However, if you're near the sea or a swimming pool that doesn't cost anything to use then swimming is a great way to get fit. Check out you community centre they sometime offer this for free.

Cycling: If you have a bike then you should use it to get fit, as well as to get around. Don't make the mistake of thinking you need an expensive bike to exercise on – you don't.

Surfing: If you're near the ocean try to buy a cheap second hand board. According to those that do it, it's hilariously fun. The board won't cost you much and should last you many years. Like cycling, **try not to fall into the upgrading trap** – you don't need a new wet suit every season or a new board just because you're sick of your old one. If someone is giving these things a way for free. Jump on it.

Snorkelling: All the gear you need can be bought for under $100. It's also amazing fun. You can make a spear out of an old broom handle and a bike inner tube. I hear it is beautiful in the deep sea or ocean snorkelling.

Urban exploration: Exploring your city, it's tunnels, oddities and bridges can be exhilarating. See what's new in your town.

Online

Surfing the internet: You probably don't need any help with this, but in case you do, here are some great ways to find new things to look at online:

1. Things to create
2. Education
3. The news
4. Video's to help you

News and current affairs: The world is bigger than your city or country. Find out about what's going on in Egypt or Syria, or learn about the political candidates in your election so you can make a better choice.

Web design: A great way to make some money on the side if you can make attractive websites or have the patience to learn how this hobby can make you decent pocket money. If you're really successful there isn't any reason why you couldn't make it a full time job. It's something you can do from anywhere and is always in demand.

Play free games online: Say goodbye to your free time. On line games are addictive so be careful.

EBay/Kijiji/Craigslist: Like the idea of buying cheap items on eBay and selling them for profit?

Watch documentaries: Expand your horizons. There are millions of documentaries on YouTube alone. If you like the odd things in life check out online channels.

Sign up to Freecycle: Another great online community based around swapping things in your local area.

Learn how to program: Learning how to program efficiently can be fun but also a valuable and marketable skill. If you're already good, check out freelancer to make some money on the side.

Outdoors

Fishing: If you can do it from the shore or on a mate's boat, it's cheap, fun and a great way to pass the day with your friends.

Gardening: Gets you outside, gives you practically free vegetables that are ten times anything you'll get in a shop and rewards patience. It's great. If you want somewhere to start, learn how to build an enclosed garden, or a simple raise bed using recycled materials. Sprout Robot will tell you what and when to plant based on your area code, and even send you the seeds.

Guerrilla gardening: The idea is to plant vegetables in public spaces in your community so that people can see how easy and fun it is to become less reliant on the supermarket.

Bush walking: Hiking, mountaineering or exploring the natural environment near you.

Camping: Get a group of like-minded people together and set off to a beautiful beach, an isolated lake or a native forest. Fun will be had, guaranteed.

Urban fruit picking: Find fruits in your community that is going to waste – but make sure you don't steal anyone's produce! The idea is to find fruit trees in public spaces that aren't maintained. Be sure to ask first if required.

Find free food in the country side: Learn what to look for; how to find mushrooms that is good to eat and source all sorts of berries you can turn into jam.

Caving: You need to know what you're doing here to stay safe. Team up with someone who's done it before. Be prepared to find an amazing world you'd never know was there. **Not for the claustrophobic.**

Social

Community Garden

Hosting board game nights: Rather than go out to watch a movie for $20, invite your friends back to your house, Monopoly or Risk.

Family History: This can take many years to do properly, and even then, it isn't always possible depending on your background. It would make an amazing present to a grandmother or relative when it's complete. There really isn't any limit on how far back you can attempt to go.

Get to know someone: Make a friend who is lonely or isolated. It could be a neighbour, or a relative who is in a home. It'll make their day every time you go.

Listen to music: This could be in the intellectual category too. Music is great and thanks to the internet and services like YouTube, it costs nothing.

Play with your children: This is pretty obvious but children love playing and their needs aren't great. Let's play in a box or kick a rock! It's all good fun and should mean not spending a cent. Teach them games from your childhood.

Play cards: There are thousands of games to play with the humble deck of cards. They are cheap and last for a long time.

Host a regular dinner party: If your friends like cooking try to arrange a regular dinner party once a month where each group shares the cooking. It's fun and cheap compared to a restaurant.

Play chess: The ultimate game that will improve your mental dexterity. You could spend your whole life getting better at this game.

Play a low entry cost sport: Athletics, soccer, swimming, orienteering, touch rugby, disk golf or gymnastics. The list goes on. It's social, good for you and frugal.

Learn to dance: Good exercises are fun. Check out videos on line, also for exercising.

Host a games night: This could be combined with different board games. It's great family fun. Can be competitive – be careful who you invite.

Videos: watching video at home is cheaper than going to the movie theatre. I call this family night with popcorn, and other nutritional things to eat. It is a great way to bond and just enjoy your family.

Martial Arts: Protecting yourself is huge.

New Skills

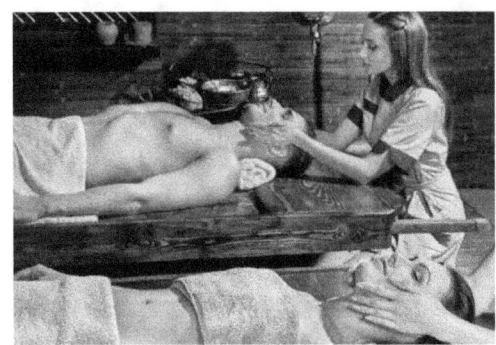

Cooking: On a normal income, you can't retire early without knowing how to cook for yourself. Learn how to cook the basics like bread and pasta and then branch out into simple, frugal meals like curries, soups and chilli. If you base your meals around frugal foods such as rice, potato and pasta, you'll save a packet.

Run a side business: Turn a hobby into an income stream. Run an online shop, create your own webpage (I did it), run a blog, do freelance writing or sell your photographs.

Dexterity skills: Juggle or learn to stand on your hands.

Scrap booking: It's a great hobby that can keep you very busy.

Craft: Sewing, knitting, dress making. Then sell it on line.

Restoration: Rebuild old cars, old furniture or anything you can find at thrift-shops that needs a bit of TLC. Make it as good as new to use in your house in place of buying more expensive items, or sell them on for a profit.

Homesteading: Learn how to live as self-sufficiently as possible. Taking care of animals and a full sized vegetable garden, but it's an amazing lifestyle if you can manage it.

Learn to sing: Voice – the cheapest musical instrument available.

Learn to cut your hair: If you have a short haircut you really should cut your own hair. It will save you thousands of dollars over the years and is really easy.

Canning: If you have a vegetable garden, then you'll end up having periods where you have way too much of a particular vegetable. The solution is to make preserves, chutneys and relishes and to can your produce to make it last.

Keep chickens: This is guaranteed to keep you busy. Having chickens probably won't save you any money, but it's a fun hobby. They are good companions and give you eggs and meat for your troubles.

Carpentry: This is an awesome hobby to have. If you don't have any basic carpentry skills you should learn them because they'll save you money. Learning how to fix and restore your possessions is huge.

Community

Volunteer your time: To a lot of charities, this is more valuable than your money. Gaining experience, networking, and potentially turn into a job.

Follow a sports team: Getting involved in local sport by watching, helping, coaching, volunteering and playing can be very rewarding.

Mentor: Many children today grow up without good role models. There are a number of charity groups that facilitate mentoring sessions. It's bound to be difficult but would be very rewarding to both parties.

Lobby: Sitting around whinging about politics is great, but doing something about it is even better. Make a difference by getting involved.

Community Garden: If you live in this country there are more community gardens there are local equivalents all over the world.

Charity Group: If you're passionate about a local issue or cause, get involved and start a group to raise money.

Organize Fundraising: If you're not up for starting a charity (which is a huge commitment) you can get involved by rising some money by having a fund raiser– a trivia night or an auction are always fun.

Boards for Community Groups: This can have the benefit of being great for your CV (*curriculum vitae*). It can also lead to bigger roles on company boards if you're good at it.

Donate Blood: One of the best ways you can spend your time. Saving lives!

Visit museums and art galleries: on a free or frugal day

Improve the Environment: It might not be the most fun in the world, but you would be doing well. Do the recycling as required by your district.

Free Community Events: Check local government websites and community boards for cheap events in your area.

Travelling

Couch surfing: Find free places to stay overseas. Be careful with this.

Bed and Breakfast: Find cheap places to stay overseas and in your area.

Travel the world by house sitting: There are heaps of good house sitting websites where you can find places to stay in the short to medium term in return for looking after someone's house.

RV: Live in a RV! *It is no*t for everyone, but if you're young and want to travel on the cheap side, this could be for you.

Become a Caretaker: Similar to house sitting although normally in remote areas and involves working for a salary.

Financial
Investing: Making a hobby of it will go a long way in setting yourself up financially for the future. It really doesn't have to be a dry subject, and is crucial to gaining financial independence.

Budgeting: I might be a huge nerd, but I love budgeting. I'll quite happily sit at home and doing my monthly budget to help me stay on track. It also gives me an idea of where the money went. Good way to learn how to cut back.

Couponing: This isn't really a big thing in Canada, but a lot of people in the US seem to be really into it. Worth a look to see if it can save you some money.

Thrift shopping: Only if it's really cheap– some stores are becoming more expensive.

Become a Landlord: Extremely time consuming, but the financial rewards are obvious. You can be renting for free. Being a landlord is a time-consuming and you are on call around the clock.

Run a Stall at a Local Market: Not a bad way to spend a day on the weekend. However, you should treat it like running a business.

Get a Part Time Job: Getting a second job that is more in line with you interests is a good stepping stone to early retirement or paying you're your debt in becoming financially independence.

Miscellaneous

Jigsaw Puzzels: It's cheap but if you look at the hours per dollar, it's as frugal as it comes.

Build Models: Not just for kids!

Bird watching: There are even organised competitions to see how many species of bird you can find over the course of a day.

Graphing Progress: If you love to make graphs and charts to track your progress towards a goal. It is really motivating, and is a good cheap hobby to have.

Dumpster Diving: I remember someone had told me that they were going to grocery stores late at night and the food that was in the dumpster in packages was ridiculous. The dates to expire in a few days – so they took them home and freeze them. **The degree of difficulty and risk is fairly high here. Please make sure you're not breaking any laws if you try this.**

The grocery store found out that people where actually doing this and put locks on the Dumpster. The food should have been given to food banks or the less fortunate.

Quit Smoking: Try giving up a habit that isn't helpful or is expensive.

Complete a List: Work through a list, for example – try to watch all of the movies you have or the entire Oscar nominated movies in a particular year.

Play Music: Especially if you're got an instrument lying around that never gets used. Put it to work and make some noise. Go on the corner and make some money.

Magic: It's good for entertaining children and is quite time consuming to get right. All the tricks can be learned from the web for free.

Build a Bunker: This and other DIY tasks around the home can be really rewarding and add value to your house.

Origami – learn this on line videos – You Tube

What is your favourite frugal hobby? If you can come up with a few I haven't covered.

FOOD STRETCHING

Eat Less

Sixty percent of Americans admit to eating more than is good for them. When you're watching your pennies, one of the easiest ways to spend less on groceries is to buy less and eat less. Start by cutting way back on snacks, the culprit behind most overeating and among the most expensive grocery items.

Focus on Value Foods

It's fun to cook with a wide variety of ingredients, but sticking to the foods with the most nutrition per dollar can get you through a lean patch. Need more options? These 50 healthy foods can be had for under a buck a pound.

Buy in Bulk

Whether it's dividing up large Costco meat packages or hauling 50-pound bags of grain from a feed store, there are lots of ways to save by bulk buying. The important thing is to safeguard against waste by making sure you have a safe place to store it and that you will use the entire purchase before it goes bad.

Do the Work

You can make your own bread for half the price of a low-end store-bought loaf, and end up with a more delicious and nutritious product. Pre-chopped and washed veggies cost a premium and don't stay fresh as long. Roll up your sleeves and do your own prep work to save.

Substitute

The recipe may call for pine nuts, but pumpkin seeds and sunflower seeds are way cheaper. Learn about more low-cost ingredient substitution ideas.

Stop Throwing Food Away

Since 40% of all food produced in the United States is thrown away, eliminating waste is low-hanging fruit. At our house, we avoid waste by serving the kids small portions and seconds (or thirds) as needed, using tiny containers to save every last leftover, and incorporating those leftovers into other dishes. There are plenty more ways to cut food waste.

Drink Water

You know by now that soda is bad for you, but you don't need juice either. If you don't like plain water, flavour it with a splash of juice instead of pouring whole glasses of juice. Not only does this save money, but it cuts calories too.

Try Batch Cooking

Assembly line cooking, once-a-month cooking, whatever you want to call it, prepping food ahead and freezing it saves money by accommodating bulk purchases and helping you avoid high-priced instant meals when you're short of time.

Rinse Out the Container — Into the Pot

Whenever I empty a jar of tomatoes or a Tupperware of soup into a cooking pot, I put a little water in the container, shake, and empty it into the cooking pot, to make sure I'm not throwing away even a gram of food. The extra water cooks off.

Learn to Make Cheap Meat Delicious

Meat lovers don't have to buy T-bones to enjoy a hearty meal. All are delicious when done right.

Dilute It

Adding beans or rice really does make a stew go farther.

Make Your Own

Prepared foods are among the highest-margin items in the supermarket. If you've never tried it, you might be surprised how easy it is to make your own guacamole, hummus, or even peanut butter.

Make Your Own Instant Mixes

Another high-cost item is "instant" anything. Make single-serve oatmeal packets, pancake mix, or practically anything you use a mix for, and save.

Consider Markdowns

"Clearance" meat section, because it feels like savings and that is what it's all about. Still, taking home items that are about to expire can save you 50% or more if you are able to use or freeze them right away.

Grow a Garden

Even if you only have a balcony, you can grow enough food to reduce your spending. To realize savings, it's important to pay attention to how much you spend on a garden. Focus on plants that produce expensive items to save the most.

Use a Full Discount Arsenal

Coupons, online deals, in-store offers, rebates — these tactics really work and can easily cut your grocery spending by 20% or more.

Switch Stores

Where you shop can make a big difference in what you spend for the same groceries. Changing from Expensive Grocery stores to Wal-Mart could save a family more than $1,600 a year. Check out the Dollars stores they sell food items also. Explore your neighbourhood — you may have a fresh produce market or a weekly farmer's market with even better prices than big box stores.

Return It

Your berries got moldy the day after you bought them? You picked up the wrong item and paid full price instead of the sale item you thought you were getting? You where charge full price for a sale item. Take your receipt and flyer with you as proof. Don't be afraid to stop by customer service the next time you visit; managers at good stores are happy to process the occasional refund.

INEXPENSIVE FOOD

FOODS TO HELP YOU SAVE

Apples – One a day keeps the cheapskate away.

Bananas – Potassium for pennies.

Barley – A tasty alternative to rice and potatoes.

Beans – Canned or dried, there are kidney, pinto, navy, black, red, and many more.

Bok choy – Steam and serve with a little soy sauce.

Broccoli – Yes, a store special. Usually closer to $2 per pound.

Bulgur wheat – Try it in pilaf or in a tabouleh salad.

Cabbage – Green, red, and napa.

Carrots – Raw or steamed; rich in carotenes, healthy antioxidants.

Celery – Stir-fry it for a change.

Chicken – Whole or various parts, on sale.

Chickpeas – AKA "garbanzo beans."

Cornmeal – Polenta is all the rage these days, but I loved it 40 years ago when Mom called it "cornmeal mush."

Cucumbers – Try peeling, seeding, and steaming with a little butter and salt.

Daikon radish – I used to eat radishes a lot as a child.

Eggs – Don't overdo them, but eggs provide high-quality protein and still cost about $1 per pound. Buy eggs for $1.99 or $2.25 on sale per pack.

Green beans – Frozen, but fresh are sometimes on sale for under $1 a pound.

Greens – Kale, mustard, and collard greens are rich in vitamins and a good source of fiber.

Grapes – Store special at 99 cents a pound.

Grapefruit – Bake with a little brown sugar on top for a healthy dessert.

Lentils – Perhaps the perfect food, healthy, cheap, and versatile for soups, salads, sandwich spreads.

Mangoes – High in fiber and vitamins A, B6, and C.

Milk –Milk is expensive so by it on sale. However, is necessary for kids growth unless they are Lactose Intolerant. Your family Doctor may prescribe a different milk or you can use Lactate Drops into the milk. Powder milk would be cheaper if they carry it.

Oatmeal – The good old-fashioned slow-cooking kind, which takes five minutes.

Onions – Try baking them whole in a cream sauce.

Pasta – Store special @ .89 a pound or less! Some time you can get a box for $1.00 when on sale and sauce also, at your local grocery store.

Pork – Inexpensive cuts frequently go on sale for 99 cents per pound or less.

Potatoes – White, red, and sweet. I just purchased for $2.00 (10 lbs) a bag.

Pumpkin – Yes, you can eat the same ones you buy as holiday decorations.

Rice – White for under $1 a pound. Brown, is a little more expensive, but better for you. Sometimes the grocery store will have rice on sale. Purchase it at that time.

Rutabagas – Never tried them. Create a meal using this. It depends on where you live.

Spinach – Frozen – or fresh. but Popeye doesn't care. Salad, smoothies, or

Split peas – Add a ham bone and make the ultimate comfort soup.

Squash – Acorn, spaghetti, and zucchini—among other kinds.

Sweet corn – Canned or fresh on the cob.

Tomatoes (canned) – Canned are often better than fresh for cooking.

Turkey – A popular bargain-priced loss-leader around the holidays. In fact, buy an extra bird and freeze it for later.

Turnips – Make me think of my grandparents, who always grew them.

Yogurt – 8-ounce containers were on sale

SALAD

Healthy and you can improvise and make changes and create your own salad.   Get creative and try these it's a great way to save money when you are on a budget.

Spicy Carrot Salad: Microwave grated carrots and minced garlic in 1/4 cup water until crisp-tender. Drain; toss with lemon juice, olive oil, salt, red pepper flakes and parsley.

Asian Apple Slaw: Mix rice vinegar and lime juice with salt, sugar and fish sauce. Toss with julienned jicama and apple, chopped scallions and mint.

Tomato-Peach Salad: Toss tomato and peach wedges with red onion slices. Drizzle with cider vinegar and olive oil; season with sugar, salt and pepper.

Creole Green Beans: Combine blanched thin green beans and red onion slices. Toss with Creole mustard, red wine vinegar, olive oil, salt and pepper.

Herb Salad: Whisk 1 part lemon juice with 3 parts olive oil, and salt and pepper. Toss with dill, basil, chives, tarragon and lettuce.

Squash and Orzo Salad: Sauté zucchini, yellow squash and scallions in olive oil until tender. Toss with cooked orzo, parsley, dill, goat cheese, salt and pepper.

Champagne Greens: Whisk 1 part champagne vinegar with 3 parts olive oil, and salt and pepper. Toss with Boston lettuce.

Watercress-Fruit Salad: Toss peach wedges and watermelon cubes with watercress. Drizzle with olive oil and lemon juice; season with salt and pepper.

Caesar Salad: Purée minced garlic and anchovies, lemon juice, Worcestershire sauce, salt, pepper and 1 egg yolk; with machine running, slowly add 1/4 cup olive oil. Toss with romaine; top with Parmesan and croutons.

Hearty Tuna Salad: Mix cannellini beans, capers, pickled mushrooms, celery and olives; stir in mustard, lemon juice, salt and pepper. Toss with cherry tomatoes and oil-packed tuna.

Panzanella: Marinate tomato chunks in olive oil, red wine vinegar, garlic, salt and pepper for 10 minutes. Soak stale bread in water for 5 minutes; drain, then toss with the tomatoes. Add sliced red onion, celery and fresh herbs.

Miso-Tofu Salad: Chop 1 inch fresh ginger in a blender; purée with 3 tablespoons miso, 2 tablespoons water, 1 tablespoon rice wine vinegar, some soy sauce and chilli paste. Blend in 1/2 cup peanut oil. Drizzle over baby spinach and cubed tofu.

Crab-Salad Cups: Mix lump crabmeat with celery, tarragon and chives. Toss with mayo, sour cream, lemon juice and mustard; serve in Bibb lettuce cups.

Japanese Radish Salad: Top a layer of watermelon radish slices with scallions and baby greens. Whisk mirin, rice wine vinegar, soy sauce, grated ginger, salt, and sesame and vegetable oil to taste; drizzle over the salad.

Jicama-Mango Slaw: Toss julienned mango and jicama, red onion, radish and cilantro; add cumin, salt and cayenne. Drizzle with olive oil and lime juice.

Tricolor Salad: Whisk 1 part balsamic vinegar with 3 parts olive oil, and salt and pepper. Toss with arugula, escarole and radicchio.

Tabouli with Pine Nuts: Mix cooked bulgur, toasted pine nuts, lemon juice, scallions, olive oil, salt and pepper; add diced tomatoes, mint and parsley.

Cheesy Spinach Salad: Whisk 1 part red wine vinegar with 3 parts walnut oil, shallots, salt and pepper. Toss with baby spinach, goat cheese and walnuts.

Curried Potato Salad: Mix mayo with cider vinegar, curry powder and duck sauce. Fold in roasted sweet potatoes, celery, cilantro and scallions; season with salt and pepper.

Smoked-Trout Salad: Whisk 1 part cider vinegar with 3 parts olive oil, minced shallots, horseradish, dijon mustard, honey, salt and pepper. Toss with flaked smoked trout, julienned apples and beets, and arugula.

South-western Cobb: Purée equal parts mayo and buttermilk with hot sauce, cilantro, scallion, orange zest, garlic and salt. Drizzle over romaine, diced avocado and jicama, orange segments and crumbly sharp cheese.

Tomatoes with Mint: Sprinkle heirloom tomato chunks with salt, pepper and sliced shallots; set aside 5 minutes. Top with fresh mint; drizzle with olive oil and white wine vinegar.

Chickpea Tapas: Mix chickpeas, capers and green olives with chopped chorizo, celery, red onion, parsley and cilantro. Toss with olive oil, salt and pepper; top with manchego.

Pasta Caprese: Mix chilled cooked fusilli, diced mozzarella, chopped tomatoes, basil, toasted pine nuts and minced garlic; season with salt and pepper.

Chicken-Mango Salad: Whisk 1 tablespoon each lemon juice and honey, some grated ginger and 1/4 cup olive oil; toss with shredded grilled chicken, mesclun greens and diced mango.

Oranges with Mozzarella: Stack mozzarella and orange slices with basil. Drizzle with olive oil; season with salt and pepper.

Dilled Egg Salad: Mix mayo, dijon mustard, dill, and salt and pepper. Stir in coarsely chopped hard-boiled eggs and diced dill pickles.

Cantaloupe Carpaccio: Slice cantaloupe extra-thin (a mandoline works best). Drizzle with olive oil and lemon juice; top with pepper and ricotta.

Three-Bean Salad: Boil 1/3 cup cider vinegar, 1/4 cup each sugar and vegetable oil, and salt. Pour over blanched green and wax beans, kidney beans and red onion slices; marinate 1 hour. Season with salt and pepper; top with parsley.

Greek Cucumber Salad: Mix red onion slices, chopped cucumber, kalamata olive halves, dill and feta. Dress with olive oil and lemon juice; season with salt and pepper.

Yellow Trio: Cut the kernels off an ear of corn; sauté in olive oil with yellow squash slices. Toss with yellow grape tomatoes, basil, salt and pepper.

Egg Salad with Beans: Toss blanched green beans with sliced radishes and hard-boiled eggs. Drizzle with olive oil; season with salt and pepper.

Ambrosia Salad: Whisk coconut milk with grated orange zest and vanilla. Toss with sliced grapes, tangerines and apples; chill. Garnish with toasted coconut and walnuts.

Cornbread Caesar: Toss cubed cornbread with melted butter, salt and cayenne on a baking sheet; bake at 400 degrees, 12 to 15 minutes. Toss romaine and chopped tomato with Caesar dressing (see No. 9); top with the cornbread croutons.

Beet Salad: Whisk 1/2 cup vegetable oil with 2 tablespoons sugar, some lime juice, dry mustard, salt, chopped onion and 1 tablespoon poppy seeds. Toss with roasted beets and goat cheese.

Celery Salad: Mix sliced celery and red onion with diced soppressata. Toss with lemon juice and zest, basil, a big splash of olive oil, salt and pepper; shave Parmesan on top.

Watermelon-Feta Salad: Whisk 1 part white wine vinegar with 3 parts olive oil, and salt and pepper. Toss with baby arugula, red onion slices, watermelon cubes, crumbled feta, niçoise olives and fresh oregano.

Creamy-Crunchy Slaw: Mix mayo with cider vinegar and caraway seeds. Toss with shredded cabbage, scallion and green apple slices, crumbled cooked bacon, salt and pepper.

Bistro Bacon Salad: Chop and fry bacon; combine the drippings with cider vinegar, dijon mustard, olive oil, salt and pepper. Toss with mesclun greens; top with the bacon and a poached egg.

Black-Eyed Pea Salad: Whisk lime juice with minced garlic, ground cumin, salt, cilantro and a big splash of olive oil. Toss with black-eyed peas, minced jalapeño, and diced tomato, red onion

Greek Rice Salad: Whisk olive oil, lemon juice, salt and allspice. Toss with chopped cucumber and tomato, scallions, parsley, dill, mint and lemon zest. Stir in cooked rice and a dash of hot sauce; top with feta.

Mimosa Salad: Toss butter lettuce with an herb vinaigrette (1 part vinegar, 3 parts olive oil, chopped herbs). Press a peeled hard-boiled egg through a fine strainer to make an egg "mimosa"; spoon over the salad.

Classic Waldorf: Whisk 1/2 cup mayo and 2 tablespoons sour cream with chives, parsley, lemon zest and juice, sugar and pepper. Toss with chopped apples, celery and walnuts.

Wedge Salad: Purée 1 cup each mayo and blue cheese with 1/2 cup buttermilk, 1 shallot, lemon zest, Worcestershire sauce, parsley, salt and pepper. Drizzle over iceberg wedges; top with egg mimosa (see No. 42) and crumbled bacon.

Curried Tuna Salad: Toast 1 tablespoon curry powder in vegetable oil; cool. Mix with mayo, lime juice, salt and pepper. Toss with canned tuna, red onion slices, cilantro and golden raisins.

Roast Beef Salad: Whisk 2 tablespoons each apple cider vinegar and honey mustard with salt, pepper and 1 cup hazelnut oil. Drizzle over endive, sliced pears and deli roast beef; top with blue cheese and hazelnuts.

Potato Salad: Whisk mayo with parsley, relish and mustard. Toss with boiled quartered potatoes, and sliced celery and red onion. Fold in chopped hard-boiled eggs; season with salt and pepper.

Daikon Slaw: Simmer 3 parts rice vinegar with 1 part peanut oil, minced ginger and garlic, Asian chili sauce, salt and sugar. Toss with julienned daikon, nap a cabbage and scallions; chill.

Macaroni Salad: Whisk 1/2 cup mayo, 3 tablespoons sour cream, dry mustard, sugar, cider vinegar, salt and pepper. Toss with cooked macaroni, sliced celery and red onion, and parsley.

Spanish Pimiento Salad: Grill scallions; chop. Toss with olives, pimientos, almonds, sherry vinegar, smoked paprika and romaine. Grill thick bread slices; rub with garlic, tear into pieces and toss with the salad.

SALAD DRESSINGS

HOMEMADE SALAD DRESSINGS

It's a great way to save money and you actually know what`s in it. Using things you have in your pantry – this is an easy ways to create your own salad dressings. Check out the recipes below and enjoy.

Classic Vinaigrette: Whisk 2 tablespoons red wine vinegar, 2 teaspoons dijon mustard, 1/2 teaspoon kosher salt, and pepper to taste. Gradually whisk in 1/3 to 1/2 cup olive oil.

Shallot–White Wine: Make Classic Vinaigrette , replacing the red wine vinegar with white wine vinegar; add 1 minced shallot.

Roasted Garlic: Slice the top off 1 head garlic; drizzle with olive oil, wrap in aluminum foil and roast at 400 degrees F until tender, 35 minutes. Cool, then squeeze out the cloves. Make Classic Vinaigrette in a blender, adding the roasted garlic and 3 tablespoons grated Parmesan Cheese.

Bistro Bacon: Make Classic Vinaigrette (No. 1); add 1/3 cup crumbled blue cheese, 3 slices crumbled cooked bacon and 2 tablespoons chopped chives.

Mediterranean: Make Classic Vinaigrette (No. 1); mash in 1/2 cup crumbled feta, then whisk in 1 tablespoon chopped parsley, 1 teaspoon dried oregano and 1 diced plum tomato.

Dijon: Whisk 3 tablespoons each dijon mustard and champagne vinegar, 1/2 teaspoon kosher salt, and pepper to taste. Gradually whisk in 1/2 cup olive oil.

Spicy Honey-Mustard: Whisk 2 teaspoons each honey and dijon mustard, 2 tablespoons lime juice, and 1/2 teaspoon each lime zest and kosher salt. Gradually whisk in 1/4 cup each olive oil and vegetable oil, then add 2 teaspoons chopped thyme and 1/2 minced jalapeno.

Mango-Lime: Purée 1 chopped peeled mango, the zest and juice of 1 lime, and 1 teaspoon each dijon mustard, sugar and kosher salt in a blender. Gradually blend in 1/4 cup rice vinegar and 1/2 cup vegetable oil.

Italian Soak: 2 tablespoons minced red onion in cold water, 15 minutes; drains. Pile 1/2 garlic clove, 2 tablespoons fresh parsley, 1 teaspoon dried oregano and

1/2 teaspoon kosher salt on aboard; chop and mash into a paste. Whisk with 2 tablespoons red wine vinegar and the onion. Gradually whisk in 1/2 cup olive oil.

Creamy Italian: Blend 1/4 cup mayonnaise, 3 tablespoons red wine vinegar, 2 tablespoons each sour cream and olive oil, 1 teaspoon Italian seasoning, 1 garlic clove and 1/4 teaspoon kosher salt in a blender. Stir in 1 tablespoon chopped parsley. 11. Lemon Balsamic: Whisk 2 tablespoons balsamic vinegar, 1 tablespoon lemon juice, 2 teaspoons dijon mustard, 1/2 teaspoon kosher salt, and pepper to taste. Gradually whisk in 1/2 cup olive oil.

Creamy Balsamic: Make Lemon Balsamic Dressing, adding 2 tablespoons mayonnaise and 1/2 teaspoon each minced garlic and sugar with the vinegar.

Basil-Walnut: Blend 3/4 cup olive oil, 3 tablespoons each toasted walnuts and lemon juice, 1 cup fresh basil, 1 garlic clove and 1 teaspoon kosher salt in a blender.

Hazelnut-Herb: Blend 2 tablespoons each dijon mustard and cider vinegar, 1 teaspoon kosher salt, and 1/3 cup each vegetable oil and hazelnut oil in a blender. Add 1/4 cup each chopped chives and dill and pulse to combine.

Lemon: Whisk 2 tablespoons lemon juice, 1 tablespoon dijon mustard, 1 teaspoon lemon zest, 1/2 teaspoon sugar, and salt to taste. Gradually whisk in 1/4 cup each, olive oil, and vegetable oil.

Lemon-Dill: Make Lemon Dressing adding 2 tablespoons chopped dill.

Roasted Red Pepper: Make Lemon Dressing in a blender, adding 1 cup jarred roasted red pepper strips and 1 teaspoon minced rosemary.

Olive: Make Lemon Dressing in a blender, adding 1/4 cup pitted kalamata olives and 1 1/2 teaspoons fresh thyme.

Truffle: Whisk 1 tablespoon each dijon mustard and champagne vinegar, 1 minced shallot, 1/2 teaspoon kosher salt, and pepper to taste. Gradually whisk in 1/3 cup truffle oil and 1/4 cup olive oil.

Maple-Walnut: Whisk 1/4 cup each mayonnaise and maple syrup, 2 tablespoons cider vinegar, 1/2 teaspoon kosher salt, and pepper to taste. Add 2 tablespoons chopped toasted walnuts.

Spiced Chutney: Whisk 2 tablespoons each mango chutney and lime juice, and 1/2 teaspoon each ground cumin and kosher salt. Gradually whisk in 1/4 cup vegetable oil.

Chocolate-Balsamic: Blend 1/4 cup each balsamic vinegar, olive oil and vegetable oil, 3 tablespoons cocoa powder and1 1/2 teaspoons sugar in a blender. Season with salt and pepper.

Cuban Mojo: Cook 5 chopped garlic cloves in 1/3 cup olive oil over medium-high heat, 30 seconds; cool. Blend with 1/4 cup orange juice, 2 tablespoons lime juice, and 1/2 teaspoon each ground cumin and kosher salt in a blender. Add 2 tablespoons chopped parsley; pulse to combine.

Ranch: Whisk 1/2 cup buttermilk, 1/4 cup mayonnaise, 2 tablespoons each chopped parsley and chives, 1 tablespoon cider vinegar, 1/4 teaspoon kosher salt, a pinch of garlic powder and a dash of hot sauce.

Light Ranch: Whisk 1/2 cup buttermilk, 1/4 cup non-fat Greek yogurt, 2 tablespoons each chopped parsley and chives, 1 tablespoon cider vinegar, 1/2 teaspoon kosher salt and 1/4 teaspoon sugar.

Bacon Ranch: Make Ranch Dressing (No. 24); add 4 slices crumbled cooked bacon.

Smoky Ranch: Whisk 1/2 cup buttermilk, 1/4 cup mayonnaise, the juice of 1/2 lime, 2 tablespoons each chopped chipotles in adobo sauce and chopped cilantro, 1/2 teaspoon each honey and kosher salt, and a pinch of garlic powder.

French: Blend 1/4 cup each olive oil and water, 3 tablespoons red wine vinegar, 2 tablespoons each tomato paste, ketchup and brown sugar, and 1/2 teaspoon each paprika and kosher salt in a blender.

Creamy Blue Cheese: Whisk 1/4 cup each buttermilk and sour cream, 1/2 cup crumbled blue cheese, the juice of 1/2 lemon, and salt and hot sauce to taste.
Buttermilk–Goat Cheese: Pulse 1/2 cup buttermilk, 3 ounces softened goat cheese, 2 tablespoons white wine vinegar, and 1 tablespoon each olive oil and horseradish in a blender until smooth. Stir in 1 tablespoon each chopped dill and chives.

Caesar Blend: 1 pasteurized egg yolk, 1 garlic clove, the juice of 1 lemon, 1 teaspoon dijon mustard and 4 anchovies in a blender. Gradually blend in 1/2 cup olive oil and a splash of water. Stir in 1/2 cup grated Parmesan.

Light Caesar: Blend 1/2 cup non-fat Greek yogurt, 2 tablespoons grated Parmesan, 1 tablespoon each olive oil and water, the juice of 1 lemon, 1 garlic clove and 4 anchovies in a blender.

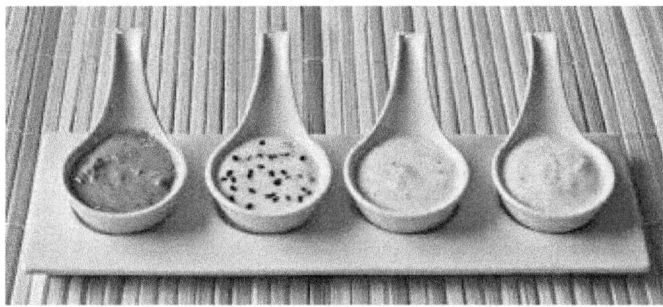

Cajun Scallion: Blend 1 pasteurized egg, 2 teaspoons each Creole mustard and white vinegar, and 1/2 teaspoon Cajun seasoning in a blender. Gradually blend in 1/2 cup vegetable oil. Add 1/4 cup chopped scallions and pulse to combine.

Creamy Caper-Herb: Whisk 2 tablespoons each mayonnaise, dijon mustard and red wine vinegar, 1 minced shallot, 2 tablespoons chopped capers, 1 tablespoon each minced chives, parsley and tarragon, and 1/2 teaspoon kosher salt. Gradually whisk in 1/2 cup olive oil.

Creamy Vegan: Pulse 2 teaspoons each dijon mustard and cider vinegar, 1 teaspoon kosher salt, 1/4 cup olive oil and 1/2 cup soft tofu in a blender until smooth. Stir in 1/2 cup mixed chopped chives, parsley and chervil.

Creamy Curry: Whisk 1/3 cup each Greek yogurt and mayonnaise, 2 tablespoons lemon juice, 1 1/2 teaspoons roasted curry powder, 1 teaspoon honey and 1/4 teaspoon kosher salt.

Orange-Walnut: Whisk 2 tablespoons orange juice, 1 tablespoon sherry vinegar, 1/2 teaspoon kosher salt, and pepper to taste. Gradually whisk in 3 tablespoons each walnut oil and olive oil.

Thousand Island: Whisk 1/2 cup mayonnaise, 1/3 cup sweet chili sauce, 2 tablespoons each sweet pickle relish and chopped chives, 1 chopped hard-boiled egg and the juice of 1/2 lemon.

Green Goddess: Blend 1/2 cup each mayonnaise, sour cream and fresh parsley, the juice of 1/2 lemon, 2 chopped scallions, 3 tablespoons chopped tarragon and 3 anchovies in a blender until smooth. Season with salt and pepper.

Red Raspberry: Blend 2 tablespoons raspberry vinegar, 1 chopped shallot, 1 teaspoon each honey.

Watermelon-Mint: Purée 2 cups cubed seeded watermelon, 3 tablespoons sherry vinegar, 1/3 cup each olive oil and vegetable oil, 1/2 teaspoon kosher salt, and pepper to taste in a blender. Add 1/2 cup torn mint; pulse to combine.

Cucumber-Herb: Make Watermelon-Mint Dressing (No. 41), replacing the watermelon with half a chopped seedless cucumber and the mint with 3 tablespoons chopped dill.

Poppy Seed: Cook 1/2 tablespoon poppy seeds in a dry skillet, 1 minute; transfer to a bowl. Whisk in 3 tablespoons cider vinegar, 1 tablespoon honey, 1 teaspoon dijon mustard and 1/2 teaspoon kosher salt. Gradually whisk in 1/3 cup olive oil.

Bourbon-Peach: Purée 1/2 cup chopped thawed frozen peaches, 1 tablespoon bourbon, 1 teaspoon each dijon mustard and cider vinegar, 1/2 teaspoon kosher salt, and 1/3 cup vegetable oil in a blender. Stir in 1/4 cup chopped toasted pecans.

Carrot-Ginger: Cook 1 chopped carrot in boiling water until soft; reserve 1/2 cup cooking water, then drain. Purée the carrot, reserved water, 2 tablespoons each rice vinegar and chopped peeled ginger, and 1 teaspoon each sugar, soy sauce and sesame oil in a blender. Season with salt.

Asian Sesame: Whisk 2 tablespoons cider vinegar, 1 tablespoon brown sugar, 1 1/2 teaspoons grated peeled ginger, 3 tablespoons sesame oil, 1/3 cup vegetable oil, 1/2 teaspoon kosher salt, and pepper to taste.

Miso-Ginger: Blend 1 tablespoon each miso paste and grated peeled ginger, the juice of 2 limes, 1/2 garlic clove, 1 chopped scallion, 1 teaspoon Sriracha and 1/2 teaspoon sugar in a blender. Gradually blend in 1/2 cup vegetable oil.

Avocado-Wasabi: Purée half an avocado, 1 1/2 teaspoons wasabi paste, 3 tablespoons each rice vinegar and water, and 1/2 teaspoon kosher salt in a blender. Gradually blend in 1/4 cup vegetable oil.

Spicy Thai: Whisk 1/4 cup lime juice, 1 tablespoon fish sauce, 1 teaspoon sugar, 1/2 teaspoon Sriracha and 1/4 teaspoon kosher salt. Whisk in 1/4 cup vegetable oil.

Peanut-Lime: Blend 1/4 cup creamy peanut butter, 3 tablespoons water, the juice of 1 lime, 1 tablespoon each rice vinegar and chopped peeled ginger, and 2 teaspoons each soy sauce and honey in a blender.

FREEBIES
FREE THINGS OR RECYLED ITEMS

EDUCATION
- Online Courses
- You Tube Videos

FOCUS GROUPS
- Focus Groups that actually pay you money
- Secret/Mystery Shoppers – company will pay you money for your experience and information

FURNITURE

- Kijii (sometimes)
- Craigs List (sometimes)
- Family (ask you family)
- Community Services- Just a tables and Beds
- Furniture Banks have new and 2nd hand items

FOOD

- Churches
- Shelters
- Food Banks

ASK FAMILY- Many household items.

- Ask Family Members
- Extended family if they have something they are not using.
- Church Family
- Community Family
- Exchanging one Item for the other

CURB APPEAL

- Furniture on the Side Walk
- Some Communities/Streets do this once a year or have yard sales
- Dumpster Diving

CLOTHES SWAMPING/DONATIONS

- Churches
- Clothes Swamping Parties
- Donated to Charities
- Dress for Success
- Clothing Banks
- Hand Me Downs

COUPONS/SAMPLES

- Help you to save money
- Grocery Stores
- Flyers
- Online – websites
- Drug stores
- Surveys which offer incentives

BABY FREEBIES/SAMPLES

FREEBEIES AND REWARDS FOR BABIES

If you're looking for some really cool baby freebies then look no further! The following links are to some of the best Companies in Canada, so you can be sure of receiving excellent some excellent baby samples, coupons, rewards and other goodies from the Companies and brands that you know and trust.

Be sure to contact the companies to see if these items are still available because they change yearly or monthly. Check to see if they have other promotions on as well.

FREE BABY REWARDS/PROGRAMS
Please check with the store to see if rules have change or if these still exist.

Huggies Rewards

Earn points whenever you buy diapers and wipes and then redeem them online for cool free stuff for baby such as toys and free Huggies diapers. The points really add up quickly, especially when you refer friends to the rewards program, too!

Nestle Baby Program

By joining the Nestle Baby Program, you could receive up to $100 in free baby products, including a diaper bag, change pad and various baby samples. You can also expect to receive promotional offers with tips and advice, plus a free baby feeding guide.

Well.ca Baby Club Get free special gifts and promotional offers when you sign

up for membership to Well.ca Baby Club. You can expect to receive up to 15% off diapers and free shipping to anywhere in Canada.

Plus, get $10 off an order of $40 or more when you enter promotional
For example Code CANADIANCOUPONSAVER at the checkout (expiry April 14th 2013). Check out the website for coupons.

Heinz Baby Club

Sign up to the Heinz Baby Club for free support through your baby's feeding development, plus a free customizable meal planner, food journal and occasional rebates and baby samples.

Pamper Village

For special promotions, coupons and offers. Earn reward points with the "Gifts to Grow" rewards program and redeem points to choose from a selection of baby stuff that won't cost you a dime. Get $50 in Pampers diaper coupons when you open an RESP through Gifts to Grow.

Similac Club

Sign up to the Similac Club for exclusive baby freebies up to $80 in value. The welcome package includes free Similac Baby samples and coupons to save money on Similac baby formula. Also included is valuable information packs on caring for your baby's development.

Enfamil Family Beginning

Receive a free coupon pack worth $30 in value, plus nutritional advice and tips. Membership includes other occasional special offers for you and your baby.

Johnson Baby---Free Guides

A library of free, downloadable, baby care guides. These are definitely worth checking out as they contain excellent information to help care for your baby. A couple of featured guides are the Baby Sleep Guide, to help get your little one to sleep through the night, plus a Bath time Fun Guide for ages 6-12 months.

Shoppers Drug Mart V.I.B

When you become a member of the Shoppers Drug Mart "Very Important Baby" program, you will receive free Shoppers Optimum Points, and a bunch of other really cool baby freebies such as advice on your baby's development as well as free product samples.

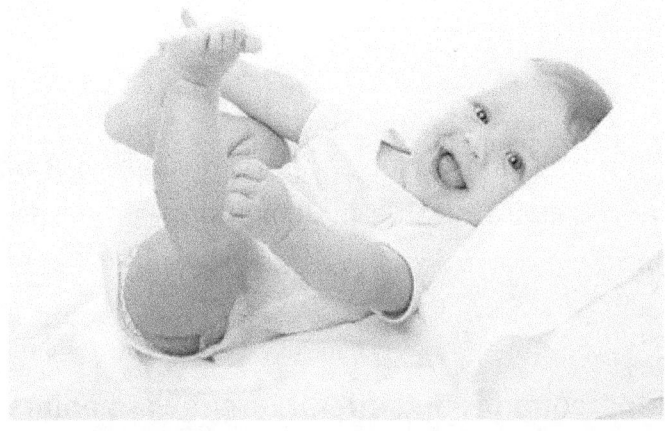

BABY FREE SAMPLES

Sometimes, Companies offer free samples of baby products on a limited-time basis.

Grabbing these freebies is a great way to try new products such as baby wipes, nursing pads, diapers, food, toys or indeed any other kind of baby product.

Since these types of offers are usually very short-lived, I post them in our Free Samples

Then, when the offer is over, I remove them from the directory so that you just get nothing but the latest and greatest deals!

FREE BABY STUFF

Please check with the store to see if rules have change or if these still exist.

Huggies Rewards

Earn points whenever you buy diapers and wipes and then redeem them online for cool free stuff for baby such as toys and free Huggies diapers. The points really add up quickly, especially when you refer friends to the rewards program, too!

Nestle Baby Program

By joining the Nestle Baby Program, you could receive up to $100 in free baby products, including a diaper bag, change pad and various baby samples. You can also expect to receive promotional offers with tips and advice, plus a free baby feeding guide.

Heinz Baby Club

Sign up to the Heinz Baby Club for free support through your baby's feeding development, plus a free customizable meal planner, food journal and occasional rebates and baby samples.

Pampers Village

For special promotions, coupons and offers. Earn reward points with the "Gifts to Grow" rewards program and redeem points to choose from a selection of baby stuff that won't cost you a dime. Get $50 in Pampers diaper coupons when you open an RESP through Gifts to Grow.

Similac Club

Sign up to the Similac Club for exclusive baby freebies up to $80 in value. The welcome package includes free Similac Baby samples and coupons to save money on Similac baby formula. Also included is valuable information packs on caring for your baby's development.

Enfamil Family Beginning

Receive a free coupon pack worth $30 in value, plus nutritional advice and tips. Membership includes other occasional special offers for you and your baby.

Johnsons Baby – Free Guides

A library of free, downloadable, baby care guides. These are definitely worth checking out as they contain excellent information to help care for your baby. A couple of featured guides are the Baby Sleep Guide, to help get your little one to sleep through the night, plus a Bath time Fun Guide for ages 6-12 months.

Shoppers Drug Mart VIB

When you become a member of the Shoppers Drug Mart "Very Important Baby" program, you will receive free Shoppers Optimum Points, and a bunch of other really cool baby freebies such as advice on your baby's development as well as free product samples.

BIRTHDAY AND PAMPERING

Please check with the store to see if rules have change or if these still exist.

BIRTHDAY FREEBIES

Many stores and restaurants in offer some pretty cool birthday freebies to help you celebrate your special day. By signing up with those companies below, you could enjoy a day of eating, drinking, and collecting free goodies without paying a single dime!

What nicer way could there be to say "thank you" to customers than by offering really cool free stuff every year?

Most of the time, to take advantage of such offers, you will be required to submit your information to receive an email alert or coupon as your birthday approaches. On the day, you should also be prepared to show ID to prove that it is your birthday and therefore qualify for the free stuff. **It's very important that you show up the day of your birthday or this offer will be invalid**.

A DAY OF PAMPERING

Some Canadian restaurants are well-known for offering birthday freebies in the form of appetizers, entrees, desserts and drinks. Denny's, for example, gives away nearly 300,000 free Grand Slam breakfasts every year to Customers who are celebrating their big day! You could enjoy a complimentary burger at Red Robin, as well as a delicious smoothie at Booster Juice. Or perhaps you may like to "treat yourself" to a Blizzard at Dairy Queen, or ice cream at Marble Slab Creamery.

Feel like getting yourself pampered? Sephora offers really good birthday freebies in the form of beauty gifts; just check out their website to see the choices. If you want some more Canadian free stuff, and feel a little retail therapy, then don't forget that RW & Co and American Eagle Outfitter's will offer you discount coupons up to 25% if you shop at their stores on your big day. OK, so that's not quite a freebie but it is certainly a rather nice birthday gift!

As you can see from the list below, you are simply spoilt for choice when it comes to finding some birthday freebies for yourself or your children! Enjoy!

COMPANIES BIRTHDAY FREEBIES
Please check with the store to see if rules have change or if these still exist.
Starbucks – Get a free drink on your birthday
Sephora – Free beauty gift
Old Navy – Join the Birthday Club and receive a free gift for you and sign up your kids too!
Red Lobster – Free Birthday gift
Veras Burger Shack – $10 Gift Certificate
Toys R Us – Geoffrey's Birthday Club from Toys R Us, free gift and card for kids under 10
Baskin Robbins – Free Ice Cream
Boston Pizza – Free Pasta or Dessert
Dairy Queen– Buy One Get One Blizzard on Your Birthday
Denny's – Free Original Grand Slam on Your Birthday
Taco Del Mar – Free Birthday Meal For Kids Under 12
Booster Juice – Free Drink (select from "Nation" menu to sign up)
Cheesecake Factory – Let Cheesecake Factory know when your birthday is through their feedback form, and you will be receive a free dessert!
Marble Slab Creamery – Join Marble Mail for special Canadian offers, updates and more! PLUS, get a sweet surprise for your birthday.

Thrifty Foods – Free 8"x12" cake child's first birthday, just drop in to Thrifty Foods

Yves St. Laurent – Complimentary birthday gift

Milestones Restaurant – Birthday coupon, dine with three friends and receive the 4th entree free

What a Bagel – Get a dozen free bagels with ID

Old Spaghetti Factory – Free kid's meal on your birthday!

Subway – Free SUBWAY SIX-INCH Sub and Drink on your birthday

Red Robin – Free Burger on you birthday

The Keg – 10oz. prime rib dinner with Caesar salad during your birthday month

RW& Co – An exclusive 25% discount on your birthday!

American Eagle Outfitters – Kids score Canadian free stuff in any 77kids store on their birthday 15% off the month of your birthday

Joeys Seafood – Join Joey's Mariner's Club for free birthday gifts

Tony Romas – Get a coupon mailed to you for a free dinner during your birth month

Narrow your search before the month of your birthday. That way, you can be sure of finding the latest and greatest free birthday treats without missing out on any opportunities! Free do change so call and see if they still offer the free of your choice. Enjoy it – You deserve it.

Please check with the store to see if rules have change or if these still exist.

REBATES
Heating Assistance Rebate Program

The Heating Assistance Rebate Program (HARP) provides help to lower-income Nova Scotians with the cost of home heating. You must register by March 31, 2016.

You qualify for this program if you pay a heating bill at your current address and meet ONE of the following criteria:

- Live alone with an income of $27,000 or less;
- Live with others and have a combined income of $42,000 or less;
- Receive Income Assistance from the Department of Community Services, OR;
- Receive the Guaranteed Income Supplement from Service Canada.

• Nova Scotia also offers financial assistance to low-income households in need of a home heating upgrade.

Nova Scotia

Efficiency Nova Scotia Corporation

Efficiency Nova Scotia, an independent non-profit organization operated by Efficiency One, has programs designed to help Nova Scotians use energy better. As the go-to place for energy saving programs and services, Efficiency Nova Scotia has programs for residential, business, commercial, industrial and not-for-profits. For more information call 1 877 999 6035 to talk with an Energy Solutions Advisor or visit www.efficiencyns.ca.

GST/HST rebates

The following is a list of rebates you may be eligible to claim for the GST/HST paid on certain property and services:

- Rebate of the GST/HST (General application, Form GST189)
  You may be eligible for a rebate of the GST/HST for various situations such as: amounts paid in error, certain exports by a non-resident, provincial point-of-sale, and Ontario First Nations point-of-sale relief.

- Foreign Convention and Tour Incentive Program (FCTIP)
  If you are a non-resident who purchased property or services related to tour packages, conventions, and exhibitions; you may be eligible for a rebate of the GST/HST.

- GST/HST housing rebates
  If you are an individual who purchased a new home, hired someone to build a home, substantially renovated your home, or leased land for residential rental purposes, you may be eligible for a rebate of the GST/HST.

- GST/HST public service bodies' rebates
  Public service bodies may be eligible for a rebate of the GST/HST paid on eligible purchases and expenses.

- Rebates for the provincial part of the HST
  If you purchased goods in a participating province and brought them into a non-participating province or into another participating province with a lower rate of HST, you may be eligible for a rebate.

- GST/HST rebate for foreign representatives and diplomatic missions (Form GST498)
  If you are a foreign representative or a diplomatic mission, you may be eligible for a rebate of the GST/HST.

- GST/HST rebate for employees and partners (Form GST370)
  If you are an employee whose employer is registered for the GST/HST, or you are a member of a partnership that is a GST/HST registrant; you may be eligible for a rebate of the GST/HST you paid on certain expenses.

- Specially-equipped motor vehicle rebate (Form GST518)
  If you paid the GST/HST on the purchase of a qualifying motor vehicle or on the modification service performed on your motor vehicle, you may be eligible for a specially-equipped motor vehicle rebate.

T2201 Disability Tax Credit Certificate

Important notice

For information on how to fill out Form T2201, *Disability Tax Credit Certificate*, definitions, examples of impairments that may qualify for the disability tax credit, and a self-assessment questionnaire, see Guide RC4064, Disability-Related Information. The Information Sheet T2201-1, *Disability Tax Credit Certificate*, is no longer available.

You can **view** this form in:

PDF t2201-15e.pdf (67 KB)

PDF fillable/saveable t2201-fill-15e.pdf (283 KB)

For people with visual impairments, the following alternate formats are also available: Large print t2201-lp-15e.pdf (235 KB)

Homeowners
Topics

- **Home buyers' amount**
  Information on how to claim this non-refundable tax credit of up to $750.

- **GST/HST housing rebates**
  Information about the different GST/HST housing rebates available.

- **What is the Home Buyers' Plan?**
  Withdraw up to $25,000 from your RRSP to buy a qualifying home under the HBP.

- **Medical expenses for self, spouse or common-law partner, and your dependent children born in 1997 or later**
  How to claim renovation or alteration expenses that improve access for persons with disabilities.

- **Renting your home**
  Information about calculating your rental income and claiming any rebate available for new residential rental properties.

- **Selling your home**
  Changing your address, capital gains, GST/HST implications, and moving expenses.

- **Provincial credits and grants you can claim on your tax return**
  Information about British Columbia, Manitoba and Ontario tax credits.

FREE EDUCATION

I said free education check it out. If you want to re-educate yourself or just upgrade this the way to go.   Lots of websites you can check out.

Below is a list of universities and other learning institutions offering free online courses. Some offer certificates; others don't. Some classes are free but there are some you have to pay for. Contact the institution prior to registering. Most of the courses are online however, some may be in person. Contact the institution of your choice.

CANANDA

1. My Slide Rule organizes online educational resources and makes it easy for people to gain real-world skills.
2.
2. Coursera is an education platform that partners with top universities and organizations worldwide, to offer courses online for anyone to take, for free.

3. **Academy** is a not-for-profit with the goal of changing education for the better by providing a free world-class education for anyone anywhere.

4. **EdX** is a non-profit online initiative created by founding partners Harvard and MIT. The site has links to Open Courses.

5. **Alison is** a global online learning community, offering free and high-quality resources to help develop essential, certified workplace skills. The site states that it offers 600 free courses.

6. **Canadian Virtual University (CVU)** is an association of Canada's leading universities specializing in online and distance education. Although the site is Canadian, it also lists courses from universities outside of Canada.

7. **Culture brings** together high-quality cultural and educational media for the worldwide lifelong learning community, and it's all free. It offers 800 free online courses from top universities. **Has over 1150 international free courses**.

8. **Toronto offers** free courses accessed via Coursera.

9.   **Yale University** provides free and open access to a selection of introductory courses taught by distinguished teachers and scholars. The aim of the project is to expand access to educational materials for all who wish to learn.

10. **Black Business Initiative Offer free course** – you must be employed or own your own business. This is not online program it's a class room setting. **Call to confirm the requirements.**

11. **MIT** has their own open courseware, where most of the materials used in the teaching of almost all of MIT's subjects are available on the Web, free of charge.

12. **Canvass Network** offer free online courses: https://www.canvas.net

13. **ADAM Offers free courses**

14. **GCF Learn Free tutorials**

15. www.skillsonlinents.ca

EMPLOYMENT PROGRAMS

http://www.ymca.ca/en/programs-and-services/employment.aspx

The sky is the limit when it comes to education especially for free.

ORGANIZING TIPS

If you don't have these items you don't have to purchase things just improvise with existing things in your home. Organizing and de-cluttering is a great way to save money.

Use old baby-food jars to hold spices. Stash them in a drawer upside down so this recycling trick looks sleek, not cheap.

Store all your instruction manuals in one binder in the kitchen or pantry.

Use a cardboard six-pack container to carry condiments from kitchen to deck in BBQ-casual style.

Keep a tray or basket on the kitchen counter where kids can drop off permission slips and adults can put mail requiring immediate action. A second tray can handle lower-priority paperwork.

Don't waste time constantly topping up cereal-sized food storage containers with dog or cat kibble. Use a metal trashcan to store one bag at a time in rodent-proof style.

Use a recharging station to keep your cell phone, MP3 player and other portable device cords untangled and your gadgets fully charged.

Can't find fresh garlic or onions? Keep them in clean knee-high nylons. Hang in a cool, dry place.

Post a sheet of paper on the fridge and note groceries and supplies needing replenishing. On grocery day, just grab the sheet and go.

Reduce spoilage of fruits and veggies by "rotating" your crops. Put new ones underneath ones that were already in your crisper.

Use small jam jars to hold cotton swabs, balls and other essentials inside your bathroom vanity drawers.

Use an old wooden stepladder to hold bath and hand towels.

Cut the amount of time you spend going from linen closet to bathroom by installing extra towel storage via a hotel-style double towel bar.

And a stash of bath towels rolled inside a basket helps, too.

Store kids' bath toys in a fine-laundry bag. Hang from the faucet 'til fully drained.

Use a shower organizer and just the basics: mild shampoo, conditioner and a body wash.

Stash extra shower products in plastic caddies – one per family member.
Keep cleaning products in a caddy, too.

Post a sheet of paper in the bathroom and note bathroom supplies that need replenishing. On grocery day, just grab the sheet and go.

Assign teens and tweens their "own" towel sets by colour. Sorting laundry becomes super-easy and sharing-aversive kids are content.
For the living room or family room, get an ottoman or bench with hidden storage under the seat.

 Large woven or wooden baskets stash clutter effectively, so stock up.

Got kids? Get large tubs that can be used to deploy toys – and quickly move them out of living spaces when company's coming. You can also use a pop-up hamper.

Don't hold on to magazines. Just rip out any pages you want to keep for future reference, keep in a file folder, then recycle the rest.

Toss dirty socks into mesh fine-laundry bags. Orphaned socks will be a thing of the past.

Dollar store plastic caddies are perfect for grouping cleaning products upright in cabinets.

 Recycle old plastic shopping bags. Store them in an empty Kleenex box 'til you need them. You can also put them in a big shopping bag and hang it in your storage area also.

Store batteries in plastic berry baskets until you're ready to drop them off at the recycling centre. You can also use this technique for compact fluorescent bulbs and orchard fruit baskets.

Big, busy family? Paint one entire wall in your mudroom in chalkboard paint so everyone can easily leave messages for one another.

Keep one basket per person in your mudroom or front entrance, so everyone knows where to drop off/find their personal on-the-go essentials like keys, bags, homework etc.

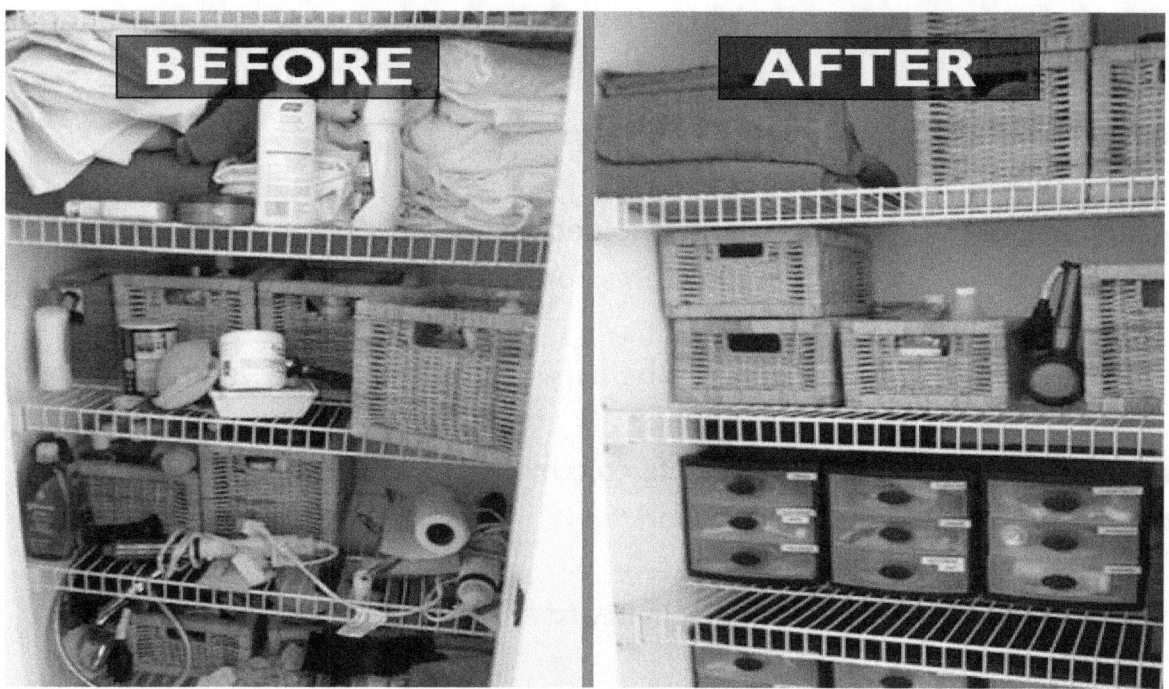

Designate a back-to-car zone by your entranceway, and put anything there that requires returning to the trunk – i.e. reusable grocery bags, empties – so the next person to use the car will remember to bring them.

In the trunk of your car you should have an emergency kit , container to put all of your vehicle cleaners, tools for the car, and keep one outfit just in case you decide you want to go to the gym or walk.

Remove the front and back from a picture frame and string rows of wire across the centre. Hang it or lean it against the wall and hook earrings onto each wire.

Easy Jewellery storage, use an old dressmaker's dolly to hang necklaces and hook earrings into. I use a dim sum 3 tier stack to put my jewellery in.

Shopaholics can put those pretty boutique bags to use by hanging them on the wall or arranging them on a shelf, where they can store scarves and belts.

Does a card run – birthdays, holidays, new baby etc. – once a year and store cards in a file tote. It's even better if you create your own card

Use ice cube trays to hold clips, erasers and other desk-drawer essentials.

Use an old wooden stepladder to hold books.

Use a pantry cabinet to put clothes in folded and saves money, storage for cleaning supplies, other household items, or school supplies.

Use white address label stickers to label what each cord in a power bar is for.

Paint an oversized canvas in one bold colour and hang it from the wall. Pin a rotating collection of your kids' artwork on it.

Post a sheet of paper on your bulletin board and note office supplies that need replenishing.

Use a canvas over-the-door shoe organizer to organize small kid's toys and art supplies.

Cookie tins can be used as an art project and art storage unit for kids. First let your child decoupage it. Then use it to hold crayons and pastels.

Preschoolers too young to use hangers with ease, install a low bar in the closet and simply drape dresses and pants across it to keep them wrinkle-free and easily accessible.

Have your child plan their wardrobe one school week at a time. Store outfits within five stacking cubbies or on five combination hangers (hangers with a bar and clips to hold pants as well as a top) to streamline their morning routine.

Keep sheet sets organized by folding and storing the fitted sheet, flat sheet and pillowcase inside the second pillowcase.

If you don't want to buy stacking shoeboxes, recycle the cardboard boxes your shoes came in by cutting out a panel at one end for visibility and ventilation. Install **a closet organization system**: it'll pay itself off with time and aggravation saved!

A well-lit wardrobe is easier to keep organized. Install a Solitude, skylight or adequate artificial light for your needs.

Don't limit closet storage to hangers. Hang hooks on the door for frequently used items.

Tackle that kitchen junk drawer problem head on. Today. Purge, edit and keep things in place with a drawer organizer.

Are you a piler, not filer? That's fine, just keep piles of paperwork organized by using folders and write-on clips.

Recycle leftover gift-wrap ribbons by using them to tie up extra electrical and other cords in your utility closet.

Dedicated tie, belt and scarf holders are closet must-haves.

Upgrade your address book for a classic Rolodex. They're retro-chic and easy to keep updated.

Framed corkboard, hang it in the kitchen and pin up favourite recipes, clipped from magazines.

Make space by putting your CDs in organizers, Recycle the jewel cases or put them into storage in the attic. **Or, purge your CD clutter** once and for all by having your CDs converted to digital files at riptopia.com. Sell or donate the used CDs.

A hotel-style hairdryer that can be installed on the wall to save space, time and energy in a small bathroom.

A pot-lid holder puts the vertical space behind a cabinet door to good use.

A wrap-organizer does the same, creating the perfect spot for plastic wrap, aluminum foil and waxed paper.

Organize vanity essentials on a vintage tray.

Use an extra wine rack to hold rolled-up magazines. I use mine to put towel in the bathroom, or as an umbrella holder.

Use cutlery trays in your drawers, but to save even more time, stash everyday flatware in a countertop caddy.

Shrink-wrap out of season clothes, blankets and duvets to save space while storing.

You'll never fit sheets back into those reusable vinyl zip pouches they were sold in, but you can stash cloth napkins in them. Use one pouch per set and label the quantity with a Sharpie. Use it to put clothes pin in.

Stash kids' art supplies on a lazy Susan so everything is easily accessible.

Organize household bills in an accordion file with month-by-month pockets.

Hold onto paint chips, fabric swatches and brochures from your last redecorating session. You never know when you'll need to reference them. Store them in an accordion file.

On your mudroom wall, hammer in two nails, then string wire between them. Provide clothes pegs and have your kids hang their wet mittens and gloves to dry overnight.

Banish tiny piles of coins and start saving in style. Get a designer piggy bank and keep it by the entranceway, laundry or kitchen—wherever you'd like to dump your change.

Tired of that circa-90s cast-iron pot rack? Move it from the kitchen to the garage or potting shed and use it to keep garden tools organized.

Get – and use – a garden hose caddy.

Edit your hangers. Choose: wire, plastic or wood and unify the hangers in every closet.

Use pillboxes to stash your earrings and rings when traveling. Zip lock baggies do the same thing.

Use a soda-can dispenser in the fridge so you can access your pop easily without tipping.

Use a wall-mounted broom and mop holder, or tie ribbon loops on the end of poles and hang them from hooks in your closet, garage or utility closet. You can just put a nail in and hang it from that.

Make a party kit. Stash napkins, extra glassware and plates, votive candles and holders, extra vases, cocktail picks and other necessities in an old wine crate and pull it out pre-party or pre-holiday entertaining so you don't waste valuable cupboard space.

Use a binder to store all medical records and information for everyone in your family, including each pet. Use dividers for each family member and include plastic pouches or expandable pockets to contain receipts and tiny record cards.

Stash awkward, easy-to-misplace necessities (extra hairbrushes, lint roller) in decorative reusable tote bags. Hang them off a doorknob in every room. You can also use candle holder or flower pots to put the brushes, toothpaste, and other things into it.

Burn digital images to CD once a month so you'll never lose them if your computer (gasp!) crashes. Or print them ASAP!

Store photos in archival-quality, acid-free boxes until you have time to organize them in albums.

Get a heavy-duty paper shredder for peace of mind – and efficient shredding without risk of overheating. Also you can use the shredding to ship things.

Place your shredder where you intercept daily mail. If that's the kitchen, so be it. Optional or in your office.

Put a small plastic caddy in your gym bag so you can manage hair care and skincare products without dropping anything. Excess water will just drain out.

Stop losing lock combinations and computer passwords once and for all. Jot everyone's codes and combinations down in a notebook and store it in your family's fireproof lockbox. You can type it on one paper and store in a safe place.

Store reusable shopping bags one inside the other.

Always keep one, foldable shopping tote in each of your heavy-rotation purses so you're never caught without. You can use this to put your coupons in also.

Avoid the last-minute drugstore run by always having a kit of your favourite travel-sized toiletries (and common OTC meds like allergy pills) packed and waiting in your suitcase. If your pills are in a pill box just take it with you (enough just for your travel time).

Get a gift-wrap organizer – wrap and ribbons, or ready-to-fill bags and tissue.

If perishables regularly go to waste in your fridge, start planning weekly dinner menus. Just buy ingredients for those meals, plus lunch basics. Post the menu on your fridge so you're on track.

 Mount a magnetized knife rack to a wall in your utility closet or basement, to keep your most commonly used screwdrivers and wrenches handy, not buried in the toolbox.

Donate your battery-powered emergency flashlights and stock up on windup models so you never have to worry about replacing batteries.

Stop stressing over the emergency preparedness kit the Canadian government recommends all families have. Just make one and get on with your life.. Obtain a list and pick these items up yourself it's never too late to start. If you have these items look at the expiration date and

Plan a closet cleanout once per season. Less mess makes staying organized a lot easier.

IMPULSE SHOPPING/RETAIL THERAPY

Impulse buying is unplanned spending where the decision to buy is made immediately before purchase. Impulse buying is normally motivated by emotional thinking where there is a perception that a purchase will bring a change in mood, such as happiness, pleasure, it's a high like a drug, and you feel better when you're doing it. It's a temporary fix for what's really going on in your life.

The opposite effect of the buyer's **remorse** and feelings of guilt following the purchase. It was once thought to only apply to small purchases, like those that appear at **the grocery store check-out**: Winners, and Grocery stores, they all have things by the cash register is to entice you to buy. Another thing is that bargain prices 50% off sales, closing down sales, or promotional deals. **We get trapped into believing we just got a deal of a life time.**

Brain Tricks and Impulse Buying
The tendency for the mind to think that current conditions are going to continue or get worst into the future and things will be the same.

New Research suggests that impulse buying also applies to large purchases like cars and houses. Impulse buying is a real psychological issue and is more widespread than anything.

This was found on another webpage about extensive research study examined more than 40 million car sales over eight years. Some of the surprising findings of the research include: These thing are truly happening and do you see anything that reminds you of yourself in the below verbiage.

- A day that is nine degrees hotter than normal saw and 8.5% increase in convertibles sold, even in winter. To support the notion that they were impulse purchases, convertibles bought on these days were many times more likely to be returned than normal.
- Houses with pools sell for $1,600 more on average in summer than in winter.
- In the three weeks following a snow storm of more than 10 inches, 6% more four-wheeled drive cars are sold.
- Less black cars are sold on hot days.

I find this a little scary but true. These are all examples of irrational purchases that are influenced by current events. **The brain expects the future to be like the present, even when logic dictates quite the opposite**. The first thing to know about impulse buying is that it is irrational and not necessarily in accordance with our long term views and plans – particularly **if you are living on a tight budget or aiming for financial independence.** Does this sound familiar?

Hunger and Decision Making
Shopping on an empty stomach is more likely to lead to impulse buying, as did making decisions in the spur of the moment. I remember when I was pregnant and hungry, I went to the grocery store to shop and I just picked up everything. My intent was to get a few things, but my mind took over and hour later I had 2 grocery carts of food. I just couldn't wait to get home to dive into the smorgasbord. I picked up lots of fruit they had in the store and made this huge fruit salad….it was so good. After I ate, I said why the heck I spent all that money.

We are more likely to choose poorly in the present because we are irrational and overestimate the value of our current feelings. Decisions are best made when we are stable and psychologically neutral (in the case of food, sated) and also when they are made in the course of planning for the future rather than made quickly in the moment.

How Businesses Trick You

Using Consumer Techniques businesses are well versed in the irrational nature of consumers and play to them at every opportunity. Infomercials exploit our tendency to make poor decisions on the spur of the moment – they only have a very limited time to explain their product and make you want it.

They play on fear (your stomach is flabby, and entice you into to buying an exercise machine); they offer you a money back guarantee to ward off lingering fears of potential buyer's remorse and have endless testimonials. They convince you that it's perfectly normal and quite an everyday experience to purchase something from the television at 3am that not even 15 minutes ago you had never heard of – let alone realized that **YOU COULDN'T LIVE WITHOUT!**

For Example: Stores will place a television that is on sale between two much more expensive televisions to make the one on sale much more attractive – despite it still being overpriced. **Sounds familiar and you think you are getting a deal.**

The list of techniques used by businesses is endless and it's important to realize that they exist before your enter a shop so that you can try to assess whether it's your irrational mind and biases taking control or whether you are really seeing good value. **Preparation and planning are key to overcoming impulse buying.**

Stop Impulse Buying/Retail therapy

 Realize that you don't know when you're being irrational. The best way to avoid impulse buying is to make it impossible. Take your credit cards out of your wallet, and don't take money with you unless you are shopping for a specific item you have already decided on.

1. **Plan purchases in advance.** Take a shopping list when grocery shopping and don't deviate.

3. **Use a 30 day purchase list for items above $100.**You can't buy the item on the list until 30 days have passed. What you will find is that you don't want the item any more, or at the very least, you've found it for much less somewhere else. Delayed satisfaction leads to greater satisfaction anyway – and you'll be much less likely to experience buyer's remorse.

4. **Make a game out of avoiding spending.** Have a budget and know how much is left in each category for the month. Learn to get a sense of satisfaction for beating the shop you're in when you leave with nothing.

5. **Watch less television.**TV is packed with advertising which is very carefully designed to take advantage of our psychological biases and irrationality. It's good at making us want things and good at making us feel like we're worth less if we don't have a particular product. Don't get caught up in the Hype.

6. **Eat before going grocery shopping.** The study I referred to above is proof that shopping on an empty stomach will cost you money. Same goes for shopping when upset. Our irrational mind can convince us that purchases will make us happy in the short term.

7. **Spending**. Knowing where your money is going is a great way to prevent future spending. Use the form provided to track your purchases so that you are aware of you spending habits.

8. **Write down your financial goals**. Have a short version of them on a sticky note on the inside of your wallet or purse so you see it before you spend anything.

9. **Be wary of special offers or never-to-be-repeated deals.** Compare prices on the internet and between other retailers before committing. It's not a bargain and it's not saving you money if you weren't going to buy it in the first place.

10. **Shop Alone.** Don't shop with someone you know is a bad influence on your spending habits. If you have a friend who has convinced you to splurge in the past – try to avoid shopping with them in the future. **You can just make them aware that you are not shopping and stick to it.**

I think making the realization that I was wasting thousands of dollars a year to impulse buying has made a huge difference to my financial future. I feel much more in control of my spending and go days without spending a cent. I stay out of stores unless I absolutely have to go.
Have you ever regretted a purchase or been a victim of impulse buying? What do you do to stop it?

AT THE END OT THE DAY DO THE HOME WORK AND GET HELP!

CONSIGNMENT VS. PAWNSHOP

con·sign·ment
Agreement to pay a supplier of goods after the goods are sold
However, if you want to get money for those things you can try using consignment it's an option to get some money back, but they also get a percentage when selling the item. **You have to sign an agreement in order to do this.**

The difference between each one comes down to:

- *When you relinquish ownership of the physical possessions*
- *When you are paid and what time-frame you will be paid*
- *The discounted price of the items*
- *Whether someone helps you sell your items*

Consignment

Consignment is when a shop sells goods for an owner. **The owner keeps ownership of his item until it sells, if it sells.** As the owner, you'd pay a small fee to the shop as compensation for them selling your item.
There are two consignment options – physical shops and weekend sales.

Consignment Shops

Consignment shops are locally owned businesses with a mom-and-pop feel. They set their own terms for how their consignments work, so it's important to research the store policies before committing. When you visit the store, the items will have an identification code on the tag to identify which account gets credit for the sale. They will provide you with a record of your items. **Keep track of what sells because it is in your own best interest. I know all about it.**

Sellers Protocol

It's standard for you to drop off your items for a 30-, 60- or 90-day cycle. If your item doesn't sell within that period, some shops will discount the item (by say, 30%), or you will need to pick it up. Find out if there is a charge if the items don't sell, which the shop collects as its profit. Some shops offer you higher percentages if you take in-store credit instead of cash.

Is it worth it?

There isn't a ton of inventory in these shops, so your item has less competition, but in many cases, there also isn't a ton of traffic coming through the door. It takes quite a while to see results from many of these shops, so it's not a great idea if you need cash pronto. I would just check with the store because some have more product than other.

I think consignment shops are only worthwhile if you have quality goods to sell. For clothing, you need to have high-end brands in most cases, however you can ask what they take on consignment. You'll need antique furniture or nearly new high-end pieces. Auctions are hit and miss.

Consignment Sales

Consignment sales are short, but intense events. They usually pop up for a weekend, 2 to 4 days, in random vacant spaces. **I've heard that** they are in strip malls, hotel conference rooms, and school gymnasiums. They are intense, because hundreds of people will be thumbing through the items throughout the weekend. The energy is high, and you can expect to see shoppers' cars packed to the brim!

How it works for the seller

The week before the sale, you'll prepare your items with tags specific to your sale (most sales have a website with full information). A few days before the sale, the organizers will open the doors for you to drop off your items. It's standard to earn 60% of the sale price as a base rate on your sold items, but you'll also pay a $10 to $15 entry fee.

After the sale, you can either collect your items or have them donated on your behalf.

Is it worth it?

Consignment sales have the opposite problem of consignment shops. There's an incredibly large inventory. I've never seen so many things in one place! Your item will have a harder time standing out, but there are literally hundreds of shoppers ready to load up their cars. **I prefer to have mine sold in the shops it's a much easier sell.**

Some people prefer consignment sale over a consignment shop, because they get immediate results. It's a personal choice.

The most important thing to know about consignment sales is that **they are only worth it if you have a large selection of things to sell**. It's hard to turn a profit with five smaller items and a $10 entry fee. Shop around for the right consignment store for you and check out the testimonials it says a lot about the company.

Pawn Shops

It involves jewellery, cell phones , and kitchen items. **I never thought of resale clothing stores as pawn shops, but technically, they are.**

In a pawn shop, you relinquish your ownership of your item in exchange for immediate payment.

Seller Protocol

For example, you want to sell baby clothes. You bring in your tubs of clothes for the shopkeeper to evaluate. At the end, they offer a quote for the cluster of items they're interested in. If you agree, then they'll pay you from the cash register. The items no longer belong to you. They may never sell the clothes, but it doesn't affect your payout. All the risk falls on the store.

I've found these types of shops to be inconsistent in how much they pay you. Your quote may be different on a Tuesday than on a Thursday for no real reason. I say this very lightly; but technically, it's 50% or less of what they'd sell it for. So, if a pair of Children's Place pants in their store resells for $7.50, you'd earn $3.75 up front. A book will resell for $10, so they pay you $5 for it.

Is it worth it?

You don't have any control over how much your item sells for. The company will make an offer, and you can accept it or turn it down. This is a great option if you want immediate, same-day results and never worry about our *crap* again. This is where you have to look at your priorities for time and money. Is it better for you to just be done with it? Or do you want to really recoup as much value out of it? **They may also require an agreement also.**

Selling the items yourself on craigslist or kijiji cuts out the middle man and all the money belongs to you.

Just research the companies and check testimonials and see what people are saying.

BECOMING A MINIMALIST

Freedom and Minimalism

You see, for a while I was happily collecting stuff: 300+ DVDs & 500 VHS (including multiple versions of the different movies!) to make sure my collection was complete, plenty of bookshelves to fit all of the videos I acquired (even if I didn't have time to watch them all), and tons of new clothes just in case I needed them.

People, like myself for a while, equate freedom with more success, and stuff. When we do that, we often add complexity, stress, and obligations in our lives – racing to what we think will give us freedom. We spend more money on more stuff and then need to find more space to fit all that stuff, and the cycle can get out of control.

Three years ago, things started to shift for me. I sold the majority of my possessions, lowered my overhead, hit "restart," and simplified my approach to health and time management. Every day is different. Compare to where I was and where I am now... is truly a blessing. **Thanking God for it –New Beginnings Life Changing Journey**. My result has been a whirlwind journey of transitioning my life one day at a time.

If you've decided this is the year you're going to improve your life, here are the areas that had the biggest impact on my journey. Pick one or two to focus on and really start to dig into it.

It's a journey but remember: by removing the unimportant, you will free yourself up for important.

1) **Simplify Your Health:** Over the past few years, I've become healthier and continue to do walking and eating healthy. I follow the same routine week after week, and just focus on getting stronger doing exercise for my back. I am a perfect example of what turning your life around truly is. Doing exercise at home or walking in the neighbourhood save me lots of money.

Realizing, if you don't do these things your body gets – your body gets all of the stress it needs to adapt and build a strong body (without spending hours and hours in the gym). Less time invested for far greater results.

The same is true with your life style change in food ethics.
Stop obsessively counting calories, weighing food, and loading up your brain with mental clutter. Don't worry about diets and supplements. Instead, stick to a few key rules:

- Eat mostly vegetables and some protein with each meal
- Minimize sugar and salt (it's in everything these days).
- Don't consume liquid calories. Drink more water
- Minimize processed food and carbohydrates. Cook and use fresh produce.

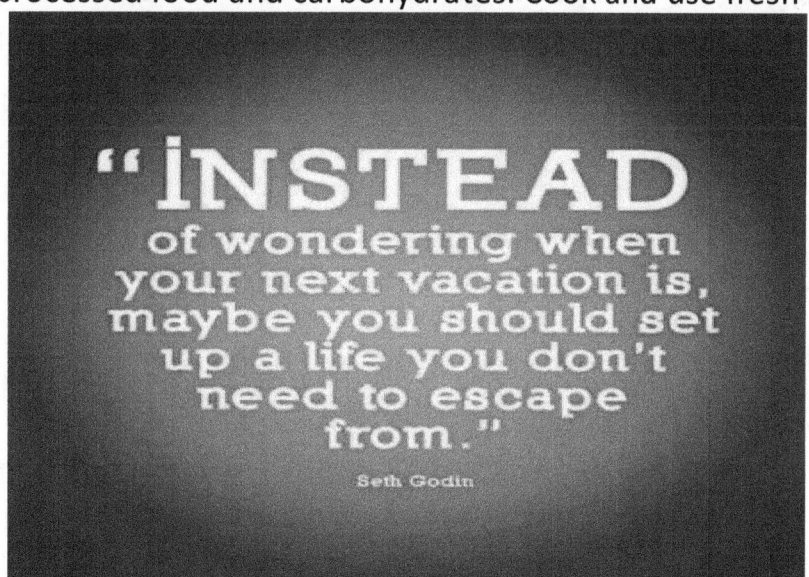

When you build a healthy body, it gives you freedom to stay off medication, spend less on health care, and fewer hours at the doctor or in hospitals, giving you more time to grow with new activities.

2) Free Yourself from Distraction: Like many people, I make my living at my computer. If I can become more productive with my time, I can do better at my job. It's tough to be free when you struggle to focus. So remove the need to use willpower to save you from distraction:

- **Remove Facebook from your phone.** Twitter and instagram too. Life still goes on. I don't use these on my telephone because I like talking to people.

- **Don't use personal websites** or add at your work on your computer, focus on your job that what you are getting paid to do during work hours.

- **Turn off notifications** or uninstall all apps on your phone that cause you to waste time.

- **Set a timer for 25 minutes** and work, followed by 5 minutes of break. Repeat until done.

De-cluttering gives you a chance to do less **AND BETTER** work.
Pick three big tasks to complete each day that will make the most impact in your business or job. Start the first task, and work on it until it's complete. Then, do tasks 2, and followed by task 3.

The unimportant but seemingly urgent tasks will continue to get in the way unless you give yourself permission to cut them from your most productive time at work to focus on the important.

3) Stop Clogging Your Life with Stuff: In 2013 I got rid of most of my possessions and left the west coast where I lived for 15 years in a different province to move back home to Nova Scotia starting over. About a month after I began my trip, I threw away half of the things I had packed and brought with me.

I had thought I had already dumped so much of my crap before I left! But I realized even going through that process I packed over double what I truly needed. Shedding possessions like this often work in layers. And much of the time, each new layer we peel to have more flexibility and freedom.

By traveling light and wearing versatile, high quality clothing, I could change plans on a whim and move quickly. On top of that, when you spend less money on things, it frees up your money for experiences.

The same is true now even though I'm settled but not without problems. However, I continue to strive for best and use what I have as frugally as possible. I had no alternative but to be consumed by it or to go with the flow and deal with it. I was out of debt but moving back here has consumed my financial wellness. Realizing I had no alternative but to use my credit card to ship things and trying to live. You may not want to make a big move anytime soon. But I challenge you to peel back a layer of stuff in your own life, whatever that looks like, and unlock the benefits of removing the excess.

4) Become Free to Grow: We all say we wish we had more time to do a fun or enriching activity, be it learning a musical instrument, learning a language, reading more, painting, taking a class, or exercising. I didn't realize there are so many free classes you can take and receive certificate for. I love that concept because it would make me more marketable no matter what my future holds.

Why don't many of us follow through on these new, fun and challenging hobbies that help us grow? Is it because we don't "***have time***?" It is because we are "**busy**?" Is it because we don't "have the energy" to pursue them after a long day.

We are trapped under the burden of our commitments and the false importance we put on things that don't matter to us. We've bought into the cult of busy – and place more value on that than we do growth.

Start small. Cancel your cable and choose to watch fewer TV shows (or get rid of your TV). Choose to stop reading and watching depressing news articles and stories and know that the world will go on regardless.

Instead, choose how you spend your time. When you viciously cut things from your life that don't make you happy or provide value, it gives you the freedom to pursue a hobby that interests you and makes you happy.

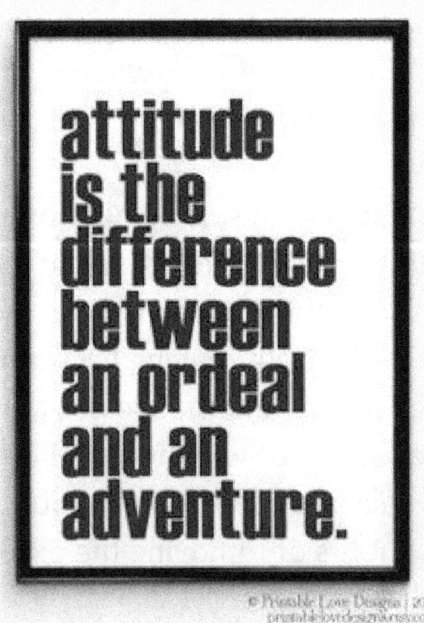

Over the past year, I started taking different classes because I thought it looked challenging and I love how it gives new insight. I only started improving when I started to focus on what is a priority right now. It's try to find full-time employment and to be ready for a changing workforce. I cleared my free time of more as a practical focal point.

Freedom is yours. Adventure, growth, and happiness are available to us. But most of us bury it by complicating our health, giving into distractions, filling our life with stuff we don't value, failing to prioritize where we spend our time.
But there's another way!

When you can deliberately choose to stop spending your resources– time, attention, and Money – on the unimportant, it frees up your resources to be spent aggressively on the things that matter.

Again, my challenge to you is to pick 1 or 2 of these areas to start, and make tweaks today to simplify that aspect of your life. Remember it's a work in progress.

Here's to a fabulous year. Remember it takes time and repetition.

THE CONFESSION OF A SHOPAHOLIC

The first step is to confess that you are and deal with it. This take time and years to get out of. I know it's like a roller coaster ride, but you must take the necessary steps and get the help you need to overcome this.

What is a shopaholic? Someone who is spending money as a result of being disappointed, angry, scared, pleasure. relief, adrenaline rush, for other problems. It's like a drug and is an addiction. I am keeping it real because I am still recovering from this. I have come a long way but still have a ways to go. Sometimes you need intervention and to get the necessary help. There was a much deep rooted issue behind the spending.

 I took the Debt Free Program at my church. I want to thank you for allowing me to be part of the team. Doing the Research has helped me enormously. So, I want to help you! All I can say is WOW! What's ironic about this is I used to work for the Bank years ago. It's doesn't matter what your profession is. Many people do it and not realizing it.

A Shopaholic is:

- Shopping/spending habits causing emotional distress or chaos in one's life.
- Having arguments with others regarding shopping or spending habits.
- Feeling lost without credit cards.
- Buying items on that would not be bought with cash.
- Spending causes a rush of euphoria and anxiety at the same time.
- Spending or shopping feels like a reckless or forbidden act.
- Feeling guilty, ashamed, embarrassed or confused after shopping or spending money. Many purchases are never used.
- Lying to others about what was bought or how much money was spent.
- Thinking excessively about money.
- Spending a lot of time juggling accounts and bills to accommodate spending.

I have experienced all of these. In fact, I used to suffer from many of these at the same time. It felt awful. An addiction to spending is a scary, dangerous thing. Like other addictions, it causes victims to feel lost, out of control.

Those who have never suffered from being a Shopaholic cannot understand the problem. They don't know what it's like to see something and feel the urge to buy it *now*. They don't know the rush from shopping, and the subsequent nausea from the guilt of having spent more money they do not have. At the height of my spending, I had a love-hate relationship with my credit cards. I knew that what I was doing was destroying my life, but I felt powerless to stop. The only thing that gave me comfort was buying new Stuff. I was out of Control.

Coping with being a Shopaholic

Based on my own experience — and based on conversations I've had with others — here are six steps you can take now to put a stop to your addiction:

1. **Cut up your credit cards.** Do it today. However, you may need it for an emergency. The card is only convenient in emergency situations with the intent to make the payment right away. However, if you have a problem with this compulsiveness, destroy your cards *now*. Just pay it off. I've done this in the past, and I know how easy it is to go to your desk drawer, pull out the numbers, and place an order online. Get rid of the cards completely. (Do not attempt to cancel your accounts, however, until you've paid everything you owe.)

2. **Only carry cash.** Don't use check book. Only use a card to pay bills online. Inconvenient? Absolutely, but that's the point. If you're a compulsive spender, your goal is to break the habit. You have to make sacrifices and adjust your attitude. Also begin to make the connection between is a need or want. There is the utmost distinction between them. ***A need is necessary, and a want is I just want to have it because it's cute***. Using cash it takes practice I know I am still learning.

3. **Track every penny you spend.** Since I took the debt free program I've been tracking every penny and it's helping me. You get see actually where the money is going. When I was addicted to shopping, I intentionally turned a blind eye to how much I was spending. I wasn't even aware of how much I spent. Lunch, retail therapy, stars bucks was across the street from where I worked. I went twice a day for Frappuccino or cappuccino and a treat. It was a ridiculous amount of money that I spent. You do the math—outrageous. I thought oh what is harm in that? Once I began to track my spending, certain patterns became clear. When I saw the patterns, I was able to act on them. I cut the amount extremely than I cut it out. Then I gradually cut it out completely.

4. **Effects on the Mind.** For some people, money is not an emotional issue. They understand it intuitively. They're able to make the smart choices without temptation to do otherwise. For most of us, though, money is more about mind than it is about math. For us, it can be useful to play tricks on ourselves.

5. **When you're tempted to buy something**, Yes, write it down. Make a wish list. I do this at in order to control my spending. This wish list keeps me from actually buying things! Eventually, you forget about it.

Yes, these are simple little tricks. But they're tricks that work. If they can help you stop spending, that's all that matters.

6. **Avoid temptation..** If your weakness is music, stay out of the record store (or de-activate your iTunes account). If you tend to spend money at big department stores, then stay out of them. Avoid the places where you'd normally spend. Seriously, it's difficult but you have to do it. I test myself periodically by going in stores a leaving with nothing... I gave myself a pat on the back.

7. **Ask for help.** Beating an addiction can be tough when you're going it alone. Seek support from your friends and family. Ask your spouse to help. (And be

open when they call you on your actions — don't get angry.) ***This is part of healing, and it's out of tuff love.***

Finally, consider seeking professional help. Don't be proud just do it—you will feel so much better. There is no shame in obtaining psychotherapy for problems that seem bigger than you. Ultimately you must look inward to overcome any form of addiction — a therapist is like a trained guide who can help you find the way.

REMEMBER THESE STEPS

Steps to take:
1. Cut up your credit cards. Do it today. ...
2. Only carry cash. Don't use check book. ...
3. Track every penny you spend. When I was addicted to shopping, I intentionally turned a blind eye to how much I was spending. ...
4. Mind games. For some people, money is not an emotional issue. ...
5. Avoid temptation. ...
6. Ask for help.

What can you do to help yourself get out of this situation? Think about it!

FROM SHOPAHOLIC TO HOARDER

As a shopaholic you can also become a hoarder and just start storing things and become a pack rat.   For those who hoard, the quantity of their collected items sets them apart from other people. I was a very organized neat hoarder who kept things in containers, lockers, closet so that they were not visible.   My apartment had everything in its place.

However, the money that I wasted was ridiculous. I remember having so much stuff that I would ship it home for Christmas and birthdays by the boxes. Well when the granddaughter came along. I would just pick up stuff different sizes for current and future. Sometimes I just gave the items out at different holidays. Overspending on stuff – having 5 lockers filled with stuff, 4 wardrobes and 4 closets, and dressers.

 As an organized individual everything had its place. Well shopping was my outlet that turned into a collection of unnecessary things.

I stopped paying full price for things when I had my daughter. I became the queen of sales and discounts.   What's bad is when you walk into a store and they know you by name telling your family you are VIP customer.

Consumerism: Stores get to know your style and size and when you come in they pick out things they know you will like. They will let you know when the sales are on, new stock coming in, etc.   When I moved back to Nova Scotia one of the stores actually gave me a necklace. The necklace is a reminder of what I wasted over the years. Well this is scary and out of control.

I remembered one time the lady in the store stopped me from shopping because she didn't want me to have duplicates. Wow, those were the days and times were chaotic. I remember purging 3 or 4 times a year, giving to charity. **I am determined not to put myself in this situation ever again.**   When you have peace of mind and can focus on what's important.   At the end of the day it's just stuff and how much do you need.

DEFINITIONS OF HOARDING

- Acquisition of and failure to discard useless or limited value possessions

- Living spaces cluttered and unusable

- Distress caused by hoarding

- Significant risk to health and safety

- Compulsive hoarding interferes with basic activities, including cooking, cleaning, showering and sleeping.

Things that people Hoard:
Commonly hoarded items may be newspapers, magazines, paper and plastic bags, cardboard boxes, photographs, household supplies, food, clothing, footwear, and pets.

Symptoms and Behavior
Someone who hoards may exhibit the following:
- Inability to throw away possessions
- Severe anxiety when attempting to discard items
- Great difficulty categorizing or organizing possessions – some hoarders are very organized.
- Indecision about what to keep or where to put things
- Distress, such as feeling overwhelmed or embarrassed by possessions
- Suspicion of other people touching items
- Obsessive thoughts and actions: fear of running out of an item or of needing it in the future; checking the trash for accidentally discarded objects
- Functional impairments, including loss of living space, social isolation, family or marital discord, financial difficulties, health hazards

Well, well, well, does this sound familiar!

Reasons for Hoarding
People hoard because they believe that an item will be useful or valuable in the future. Or they feel it has sentimental value, is unique and irreplaceable, or too big a bargain to throw away. They may also consider an item a reminder that will jog their memory, thinking that without it they won't remember an important person or event. Or because they can't decide where something belongs, it's better just to keep it.

Compulsive Hoarding
Hoarding disorder is where someone acquires an excessive number of items and stores them in a chaotic or neat manner. The items can be of little or no use at the time-they believe in having things just in case, you fill in the blank.

The behavior usually has deleterious effects—emotional, physical, social, financial, mentally, and so much more.
1. Compulsive hoarding affects approximately millions of people in a Country.
2. Compulsive hoarding is often considered a form of Obsessive-Compulsive Disorder because between 18 and 42 percent of people with OCD experience some compulsion to hoard. However, compulsive hoarding can affect people who don't have OCD.

4. The compulsion to hoard often starts during childhood or the teen years, but doesn't usually become severe until adulthood. However, some of these habits are taught over the years.

5. Hoarding can be more about fear of throwing something away than about collection or saving. Thinking about discarding an item triggers anxiety in the hoarder, so she hangs on to the item to prevent angst.

6. Many hoarders are perfectionists. They fear making the wrong decision about what to keep and what to throw out, so they keep everything.

7. Hoarding often runs in families and can frequently accompany other mental health disorders, like depression, social anxiety, bipolar disorder, and impulse control problems. A majority of people with compulsive hoarding can identify another family member who has the problem.

8. Compulsive hoarders rarely recognize their problem. Generally, only after the hoarding becomes a problem with other family members is the problem discussed.

9. Compulsive hoarding can be difficult to control. It is usually treated in the same way OCD is. However, compulsive hoarding doesn't usually respond as well as other kinds of OCD.

Getting the help to get you out of hoarding is very important. When you have a place with less, no junk, you feel rejuvenated.
For those suffering from the hoarding condition, dealing with the stresses that come along with living in such debilitating conditions can be overwhelming. Finding a *Hoarder Cleaner* or family members that can help to sanitize the home, but also helps organize and sort through the items in all affected areas, this is crucial for a successful recovery. You should just do it yourself as part of your therapy and feel relief.

The physical threats of the hoarding. Certain physical dangers are common like:
- Being trapped under fallen piles and stacks of hoarded items or debris
- Exposure to poisons and/or bio-hazards (feces, vomit, urine, etc.)
- Exposure to spoiled or rotten food products
- Insect infestation
- Mold and Mildew

- Ending up with serious Health problems
-

Mental and emotional burdens can also wreak havoc on the life of someone suffering from the hoarding condition. Mental and emotional anguish can manifest itself physically. By taking this first step on the road to recovery, hoarders and their loved ones can avoid the irreparable damage that comes along with quarrelling about the hoarded home.

If hoarders are not fortunate enough to have helpers, it may be because they have distanced themselves socially from friends and loved ones. Social dangers such as self-imposed isolation can cause extreme depression and loneliness.

Chaotic Hoarder

Living Room

Before

After

Extreme Hoarder

Neat Hoarder

<u>STEPS TO STOP HOARDING</u>

1. IS IT REALLY USEFUL?

One of the most important ways to stop hoarding is to avoid bringing new objects into the house. Every time you are tempted to shop, stop and think for a moment. Ask yourself if you need it, if you'll use it, and do you already have one? Chances are you don't actually need it, and it will sit in a cupboard unused. So leave it on the shelf!

2. FLEA MARKET FAILURE

We all love a bargain, but flea markets and garage sales are a disaster area where hoarders are concerned. All those lovely things looking for a new home, and for just 50c or a dollar! If you're a flea fan, either limit your budget or go with specific items in mind. And don't forget to ask yourself the same questions in point 1 before you buy!

3. JUST SAY NO

Some hoarders are basically a home for everyone else's junk. Do you get offered unwanted goods by your neighbours/friends/ family? The danger is when you either feel obliged to accept a 'gift', or hate to see something thrown away. It's not your problem that they want to dispose of something. Just say no, thanks.

4. ASK YOURSELF WHY

It's also very important to look at the reasons behind your hoarding. Is it because you shop when you're bored? Does having possessions around you make you feel less lonely? Whatever your motives for hoarding, you need to know what they are, and resolve to deal with them.

5. TOTAL COST

If you want to know how to stop being a hoarder, this tip can be very effective. Work out roughly how much you've spent on possessions in the last year, say, or the value of the goods in just one room. It doesn't have to be a precise figure, but the total will probably astound you. Now, wouldn't that money have been better in the bank? This may just break the urge to acquire more 'stuff'.

6. RUTHLESS REGULARITY

The reformed hoarder has to take great care not to fall back into their old ways. So once you've managed to get on top of your hoarding, learn to keep your shopping cravings under control. In addition, if you do buy new things, find a new home for old ones. Regularly sort through your possessions and discard anything that you've used up or no longer need.

7. ACCEPT HELP

If you want to stop hoarding but feel overwhelmed by the task ahead, ask a friend for help. Choose someone who is capable of being tough, and don't query every time they want to throw something out. A friend can be very useful in giving you honest opinions, especially when it comes to pruning a bulging wardrobe of clothes that don't suit you!

8. ORGANIZE

Finally, get your possessions organised. This is where a friend can again be very useful. Storing everything properly makes them easier to find, keeps them tidy, and makes life less stressful. When possessions have their place, your home looks a lot better in a designated spot.

When you want to stop hoarding, it's bound to be a challenge. However, it's worth the effort of working on it, so that you can live in a stress-free, tidy home. You can't relax if your house is crammed to the rafters, and too many possessions not only occupy space, but also your energy.

Have you any other effects tips on how to stop being a hoarder?

www.ingramcontent.com/pod-product-compliance
Lightning Source LLC
Chambersburg PA
CBHW080702190526
45169CB00006B/2206